Lake Placid

by

Michaela Gaaserud

Lake Placid (*Tourist Town Guides®*)
© 2011 by Michaela Gaaserud
Published by: Channel Lake, Inc., P.O. Box 1771, New York, NY 10156-1771
http://www.touristtown.com

Author: Michaela Gaaserud
Copyeditor: Kate St. Clair
Cover Design: Julianna Lee
Maps: Eureka Cartography
Page Layout Design: Mark Mullin
Publisher: Dirk Vanderwilt

Front Cover Photos:
"Whiteface Ski Area" © Michaela Gaaserud
"Lake Placid" © iStockphoto.com
"Kayak" © iStockphoto.com
Back Cover Photo:
"Ski Jump" © iStockphoto.com

Published in April 2011

3 4015 07112 9991

ISBN-13: 978-1-935455-15-8

Disclaimer: The information in this book has been checked for accuracy. However, neither the publisher nor the author may be held liable for errors or omissions. *Use this book at your own risk.* To obtain the latest information, we recommend that you contact the vendors directly. If you do find an error, let us know at corrections@channellake.com.

Channel Lake, Inc. is not affiliated with the vendors mentioned in this book, and the vendors have not authorized, approved or endorsed the information contained herein. This book contains the opinions of the author, and your experience may vary.

Help Our Environment!

Even when on vacation, your responsibility to protect the environment does not end. Here are some ways you can help our planet without spoiling your fun:

★ Ask your hotel staff not to clean your towels and bed linens each day. This reduces water waste and detergent pollution.

★ Turn off the lights, heater, and/or air conditioner when you leave your hotel room.

★ Use public transportation when available. Tourist trolleys are very popular, and they are usually cheaper and easier than a car.

★ Recycle everything you can, and properly dispose of rubbish in labeled receptacles.

Tourist towns consume a lot of energy. Have fun, but don't be wasteful. Please do your part to ensure that these attractions are around for future generations to visit and enjoy.

How to Use this Book

Attractions are usually listed by subject groups. Attractions may have an address, Web site (🖱), and/or telephone number (☎) listed.

Must-See Attractions: Headlining must-see attractions, or those that are otherwise iconic or defining, are designated with the ⭐ **Must See!** symbol.

Coverage: This book is not all-inclusive. It is comprehensive, with many different options for entertainment, dining, and shopping, but there are many establishments not listed here.

Prices: At the end of many attraction listings is a general pricing reference, indicated by dollar signs, relative to other attractions in the region. The scale is from "$" (least expensive) to "$$$" (most expensive). Contact the attraction directly for specific pricing information.

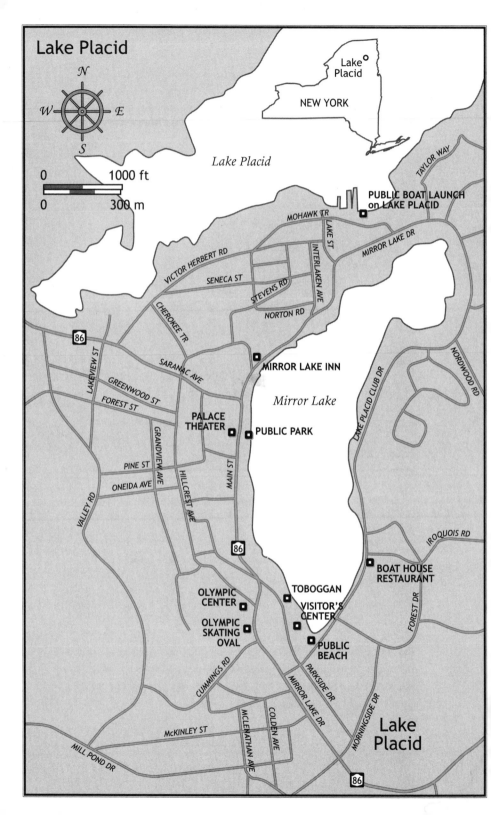

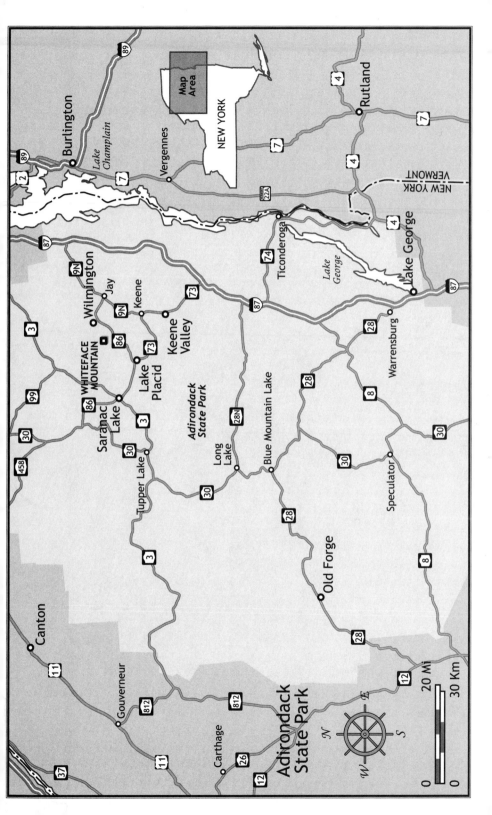

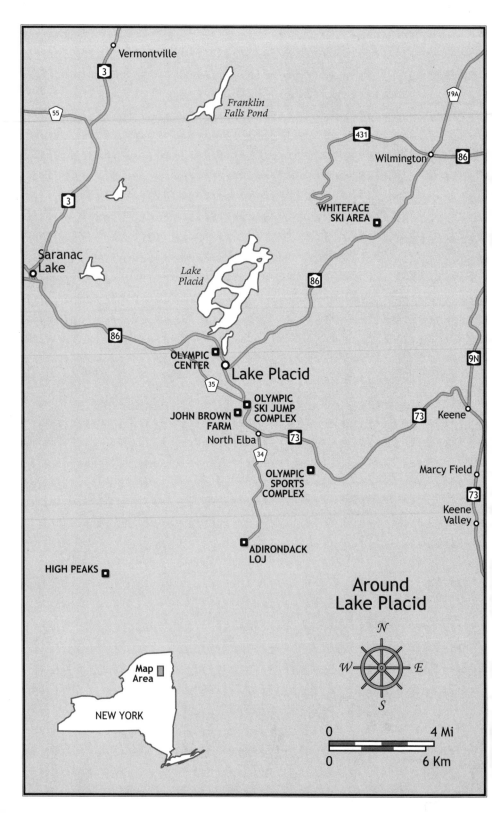

Table of Contents

Introduction 11
    Saranac Lake & Other Adirondack Towns 13
Lake Placid History 15
Area Orientation 23
    Getting to Lake Placid 24
    By Car 24
    By Bus 25
    By Air 26
    By Train 27
    Getting Around 28
    Medical and Emergency Services 30
Olympic Venues 31
    Olympic Center 31
    Olympic Jumping Complex 34
    Other Areas of Olympic Interest 35
Attractions 37
    Museums and Learning Centers 37
    Tours 42
    Arts and Music 44
    Family Fun 47
    Festivals 48
Lodging 55
    Lodging on Main Street 56
    Accommodations Off Main Street 60
    Surrounding Area Lodging 66
    Camping 69
    Rental Homes/Camps 74
Dining 75
    Main Street Restaurants 75
    Restaurants Off Main Street 80
    Surrounding Area Restaurants 87

Shopping and Retail Services 91
    Specialty Stores and Boutiques..............................91
    Specialty Food Stores 97
    Gifts and Souvenirs 100
    Arts and Craft Galleries...101
    Adirondack Furnishings 103
    Farmers Markets 106
    Spas and Salons...107
    Outdoor Gear and Guiding 108
Summer Activities 111
    Boating 111
    Bird Watching..113
    Climbing and Mountaineering..............................114
    Cycling (Road)..116
    Fishing..117
    Golf 119
    Hiking...121
    Mountain Biking 124
    Paddle Sports...126
    Whiteface Mountain..128
    Horseback Riding 129
    Scenic Railroad Rides 130
    Tennis 131
    Other Summer Activities...131
Winter Activities 133
    Cross-Country Skiing...133
    Dog Sledding 134
    Downhill Skiing and Snowboarding.....................135
    Hockey and Skating...138
    Snowmobiling 139
    Other Winter Activities...140

Sporting Events 143
    Spring Events 143
    Summer Events..144
    Fall Events 149
    Winter Events 151
Lake George...153
    Accommodations......................................154
    Camping..158
    Dining..160
    Attractions 164
    Beaches...169
    Festivals and Events 170
Old Forge..173
    Accommodations......................................174
    Camping..176
    Dining..177
    Attractions and Activities 180
    Festivals and Events 183
Index 187

About the Author

An avid outdoor enthusiast and part-time Adirondack resident, Michaela Gaaserud is always eager to try new activities and learn about the history and unique aspects of the park. A longtime travel writer, Michaela has written for newspapers, magazines and national publications such as *Canoe & Kayak Magazine* and *Paddler Magazine*. This is her second guidebook.

For Mom and Dad
Glad you are enjoying the Adirondacks!

Introduction

Lake Placid is best known as an Olympic city, earning this title as host to the Winter Olympic Games in 1932 and then again in 1980. While the Olympics introduced Lake Placid to the world as a winter sports playground, the town is truly a year-round destination with amazing and unique attractions during all four seasons.

Lake Placid is located in Adirondack State Park. The park was created in 1892 and is the largest publicly protected land in the lower 48. It encompasses six million acres and has more than 3,000 lakes and 30,000 miles of streams and rivers. The park is made up of approximately half "forever wild" state-protected land and half privately owned land. Both are regulated by the Adirondack Park Agency, which was created in 1971 to develop long-range plans for all land use in the park. The result is a protected area similar in size to the state of Vermont and more than twice as large as Yellowstone National Park.

Lake Placid is located in the north central Adirondacks, less than two hours by car from the Canadian border and five hours from New York City. It sits in the shadows of the High Peaks and is surrounded by the Sentinel Range Wilderness to the east, the High Peaks Wilderness to the south and the McKenzie Mountain Wilderness to the north. To the west are the small town of Ray Brook and the better-known town of Saranac Lake.

Lake Placid offers a fine blend of sports, culture, outdoor activities and amazing scenery. One of the nation's best locations for outdoor recreation, a wide variety of interests can be satisfied here. The village has less than 3,000 fulltime residents and draws more than 1.8 million visitors each year.

The village sits on the shores of Mirror Lake and Lake Placid, and overlooks the Sentinel Range. A mix of quaint shops, restaurants, small hotels and outlet stores line the Main Street. With the exception of the outlets, most stores are independently owned and operated.

Winter in Lake Placid is magical. As snow blankets the countryside, athletes from around the globe flock to town to face off at the Olympic venues. World-class competition in events such as downhill skiing, luge, bobsled, hockey and ski jumping take place all winter. Most events are open to the public for a small fee, or visitors can take advantage of the fantastic facilities and participate in numerous winter sports themselves. Local festivals and holiday celebrations are also a big draw for Lake Placid, and the town is in full swing throughout the winter season.

The spring thaw brings the maple run, the time when local maple trees are tapped and sugarhouses jump into action to make delicious syrup. The season also marks the start of fly-fishing season in the Adirondacks, and spring bird watching draws more and more visitors each year. Numerous events are also held at the **Lake Placid Center for the Arts** including concerts, film showings and local art shows. The CAN/AM Hockey Tournament is another popular springtime event that draws visitors from both sides of the border.

Summer is the most popular season to visit Lake Placid. The town hosts events nearly every weekend including the famous **Lake Placid Horse Show** and the **I Love New York Horse Show**, and the **Ironman USA** triathlon. Farmers markets and festivals open around the region, and people from all over the world come to the Adirondacks for outdoor activities such as canoeing, hiking, golf, rock climbing, road biking, mountain biking, kayaking and camping. The pleasant temperatures and low humidity provide a nice break from the summer heat for many East Coasters. More than a million visitors come from all over the world to enjoy the summer activities offered in Lake Placid.

Few regions can compete with the fall foliage in Lake Placid. Bright cloudless skies frame millions of brilliantly colored trees across the unspoiled mountains. "Leaf peepers" fill hotels, camps, bed and breakfasts and the many lodges throughout the area. The crisp air smells of a mix of campfire and evergreens as the days start to get shorter. Several well-known events take place in and near Lake Placid in the fall, including **Oktoberfest** at the **Whiteface Ski Area**, the **Adirondack Canoe Classic** (a 90-mile paddling race) and the **Whiteface 5K Downhill Mountain Bike Race**.

Truly a four-season tourist town, Lake Placid offers something unique to visitors all year. Although the outdoor grandeur is the dominant force in the Adirondacks, Lake Placid's history, shopping, world-class athletics and wide selection of accommodations easily puts it on the map as a great travel destination.

SARANAC LAKE & OTHER ADIRONDACK TOWNS

Adirondack State Park is enormous. It can take several hours to drive from one end to the other and many beautiful small towns are nestled along rivers, tucked into mountain valleys and border pristine lakes. Two towns in particular, Lake George and Old Forge are tourist centers in their own right and are each located approximately two hours by car (in different directions) from Lake Placid. Each has a chapter dedicated to it in this book.

Several towns are located less than 20 miles from Lake Placid—Saranac Lake, Wilmington (home of **Whiteface Mountain**), and Keene Valley (in the High Peaks). They are easily accessible from Lake Placid and offer unique attractions, activities and establishments that are also included in this book. Saranac Lake could be considered Lake Placid's sister village, since it is located just seven miles west of Lake Placid on Route 86. Like Lake Placid, Saranac Lake sits on the shore of a lake that isn't its namesake (Lake Flower), but is in close proximity to the Saranac Lakes (Lower Saranac, Middle Saranac and Upper Saranac). The similarities, however, end there. Where Lake Placid is primarily a tourist town, Saranac Lake is a working town and has the largest permanent population in the Adirondacks. That isn't to say that Saranac Lake doesn't have a lot to offer visitors. It is a beautiful and historic town that was named an All-America City by the National Civic League—and was also named by the *New York Post* as one of the "top 100 summer destinations."

Saranac Lake was first settled in 1819, but in 1876, the town turned into something unique—a cure center for tuberculosis. Most visitors and residents arrived by train and many sanatoriums and "cure houses" were built to accommodate patients. After the discovery of penicillin, the need for cure houses diminished, but their roots remain an important part of the town's heritage. Saranac Lake has 186 buildings listed on the National Register of Historic Places.

Because of its close proximity to Lake Placid, many establishments and activities in Saranac Lake are included in this book.

Lake Placid History

It's hard to mention Lake Placid without thinking of the Olympics. Although the Olympics are a big part of the history of the Village of Lake Placid, many other influences helped shape this thriving resort community.

GEOLOGY

Most of the High Peaks surrounding Lake Placid are made up of the rock anorthosite. Oddly, this rock is normally found deep underground but is also prevalent on the moon. These rocks, and others composing the Adirondack region are some of the oldest on Earth (approximately one billion years old).

Most of the prominent features in the Adirondack landscape are a direct result of the last Ice Age, which ended about 10,000 years ago, and a slow uplift that is several million years old. The large boulders found in the Adirondacks that are sometimes in unexpected places such as the top of a mountain or the middle of a field were picked up by the moving glaciers and then left behind when the ice receded. This ice movement resulted in the formation of the many lakes and ponds in the Adirondacks, and produced the numerous waterfalls and rapids throughout the park.

There are more than 100 summits in the Adirondacks. Their heights range from less than 1,200 feet to more than 5,000 feet. Mount Marcy is the highest peak, standing 5,344 feet. The tallest mountains are part of the 46 Peaks—those with an altitude over 4,000 feet. Many hikers each year aspire to climb the 46 Peaks, and references to the peaks are found in local establishments on shirts, on signs and as names of menu items.

THE EARLY YEARS

The first people to live in the Adirondacks came about 10,000 years ago. They settled along Lake Champlain, which at the time was a sea. It is believed that Algonquin groups later came to the Adirondacks to hunt, fish and collect native plants. Following on their heels were farming groups from neighboring river valleys such as the St. Lawrence and Mohawk who came to take advantage of the plant and animal resources.

It is believed that the name *Adirondack* may have meant "barkeater," and was a term used to describe the Algonquin people who were sometimes forced to eat tree bark when food was scarce.

THE ARRIVAL OF SETTLERS

The first settlers on record to come to the area, now known as Lake Placid, were a Revolutionary War veteran named Elijah Bennet and his wife, Rebecca. The couple arrived by oxen cart from Vermont in 1800. Soon after, other pioneers arrived, and by 1810, nearly 200 people had settled in the area.

The area around the Village of Lake Placid was originally named the Town of North Elba in the early 19th century. At the time, the Adirondacks were primarily known for their timber and iron resources. Iron ore was discovered in the North Elba area and for a few short years, the Elba Iron Steel Manufacturing Company operated an ironworks complex there. During the War of 1812, the company fulfilled many government contracts in support of the war, but shortly after, business dropped and the complex closed. Later it was used as a sawmill, but only a sparse population remained permanent residents of the area.

In the mid-1800s, a wealthy landowner named Gerrit Smith turned over large tracts of land around North Elba to former slaves to help establish them as voting citizens. Hearing about this, famous abolitionist John Brown purchased land from Smith to build a farm and provide guidance to the new land-owners. John Brown's farm still stands as a historic landmark near the ski jump complex and is also his final resting place.

TRANSFORMATION TO A RETREAT DESTINATION

In the late 1800s, with the introduction of the railroad to the North Country, the wealthy discovered the Adirondacks as a retreat area. Many began constructing large rustic compounds out of local timber and stone. These compounds were later called "Great Camps," and several of them still remain under both private and public ownership. Great Camps were used for vacation, entertaining, hunting and fishing.

At the same time, the first public lodgings began to spring up to accommodate tourists.. At the time, what is now known as Mirror Lake was called Bennet's Pond. It was renamed in 1870 after a visitor referred to the pond as Mirror Lake in a hotel register.

To put things in perspective, in 1880 the heart of what is now the village was a pastoral landscape along Mirror Lake. The present day Main Street was merely a cow path running along the lakeshore.

In the 1870s and 1880s, a series of grand hotels were built specifically for summer use. Unfortunately, most were destroyed by fire—a fate that still plagues many historic and modern-day Adirondack establishments, due to the use of wooden building materials and wood burning stoves.

One hotel that survived the era was the Grandview Hotel. It was located where the present-day **Crowne Plaza** sits overlooking Main Street, and was best known for its gourmet food and dance bands. The building finally closed in 1956 and was demolished in the early 1960s.

THE LAKE PLACID CLUB

In 1895, the Lake Placid Club was established. The club began with 30 members, one building and five acres of land. Although it went through several name changes and had good and bad times, the club remained the center of recreation and entertainment for almost 100 years. At its height, the club spanned 10,600 acres with 360 buildings and accommodated more than 1,400 guests. The Lake Placid Club was the first to stay open all winter and as such, forwarded interest in winter sports in North Elba.

In 1919, the first major international speed skating competition was held on a newly built speed skating oval (the Eastern Outdoor Championships), and by the 1920s, additional facilities were built to accommodate winter athletes including a ski jump. This infrastructure contributed to the decision by the International Olympic Committee (IOC) to hold the 1932 Winter Olympic Games here. The club served as headquarters for the IOC during those games.

In 1900, the town incorporated as the Village of Lake Placid. Prior to the Olympic Games, the Lake Placid Club founder, Melvil Dewey (who also invented the Dewey Decimal System), provided the inspiration for the village to change its name to Lake Placid. The Village of Lake Placid is currently located in the Town of North Elba, which makes up the North Elba/ Lake Placid Region. Lake Placid is also located in Essex County.

THE OLYMPIC ERA

By the time the Olympics came to Lake Placid, the little village had grown into a summer resort destination and a winter sports hot spot. The Lake Placid Club hosted more than 80 competitions a year and provided funding for youths to compete abroad.

The Adirondacks were at the height of the Great Camp Era, and vacationers who didn't have their own stone and timber mansions enjoyed the area from a variety of large hotels, boarding houses and inns.

The 1932 Olympics brought worldwide recognition to Lake Placid and helped cement its reputation as a winter sports mecca. Although the Olympics took place during the Great Depression, 350 athletes representing 17 countries participated. The governor of New York, Franklin D. Roosevelt, opened the games. By the end of the first day, two gold speed skating medals were awarded to Lake Placid's own Jack Shea, who was the first athlete to win two gold medals in one Olympics. This was just the first of many historic Olympic moments in Lake Placid.

The Lake Placid Club continued to provide recreation to its members after the Olympics. Between 1940 and 1970, the club was in its prime and supported a continual flow of guests to its facilities. During this time, Lake Placid began to draw more and more attention and the number of visitors grew substantially. Music, art and theatre became more prominent, and the **Lake Placid Center for the Arts** opened in 1972.

The Winter Olympic Games returned to Lake Placid in 1980, this time in the middle of the Cold War. Only three locations have hosted two Winter Olympics: Lake Placid; St. Moritz, Switzerland; and Innsbruck, Austria. Many upgrades were made to the athletic facilities prior to the Olympic return. The **Olympic Center** was expanded with two new arenas, the first artificial snow machine to be used for Olympic competition was installed at **Whiteface Mountain**, and a new ski jumping complex was built.

Because of a lack of funding, the federal government backed the construction of the Olympic Village. The deal was that the village would be converted to a medium-security federal correctional institution after the games ended. The village was built off Route 86, halfway between Lake Placid and Saranac Lake. The institution is still in operation today and provides valuable jobs for area residents.

The high school in Lake Placid overlooks the speed skating oval and was used as the press center for the 1980 Winter Olympics. The school was issued a liquor license to serve drinks at three private lounges inside. It is the only high school in the nation to have held a liquor license.

The 1980 Winter Olympics had many historical moments. There are two, however, that will forever be remembered. The first is the "miracle" hockey game where a very young U.S. team made up of amateur players with an average age of just

22, defeated the heavily favored Soviet Union national hockey team. The Soviets were universally considered the best hockey team in the world. The U.S. team's amazing 4–3 win is widely considered to be the best Olympic victory of all time. "Miracle on Ice," as the win is referred to, led to the gold medal game where the U.S. defeated Finland.

The second historical moment was when U.S. speed skater Eric Heiden captured an unprecedented five individual gold medals in as many events. Heiden is considered by many to be the best speed skater in the sport's history, since he captured multiple gold medals in both sprint and distance events.

LAKE PLACID TODAY

Although Lake Placid prides itself on a historic Olympic past, visitors come from around the globe to enjoy its natural surroundings, performing arts, festivals, shopping, dining and a broad array of year-round sports.

Visiting Lake Placid is like traveling back in time but with all the modern conveniences. Vintage Chris-Craft wooden boats can be seen streaming across pristine lakes in summer while cross-country skiers dot the snowy countryside in winter. Because much of the land in the Adirondacks is protected, the mountains remain an unspoiled landscape with only minimal intrusion from man. The atmosphere is much as it was when the village was originally founded.

Both hunting and fishing are allowed in the park, but strict regulations are enforced to avoid overfishing and the depletion of natural resources. The result is an abundance of trout and black bass, among other types of fish, in rivers, lakes and ponds. Hunting and fishing licenses are available from the Town Clerk's office on Main Street in Lake Placid.

Traditional timber buildings with handcrafted railings and birch bark detailing are common in the Village of Lake Placid, and the rustic style of furnishings and interior design lives as much today as it did more than a century ago. Although many visitors come from large, fast-paced cities, the "speed" in Lake Placid is taken down a notch or two. Cars actually stop for pedestrians in crosswalks, dogs are welcome in many establishments, and the people for the most part go out of their way to be helpful.

Area Orientation

★

Lake Placid is known as a great family destination. It is also known in the athletic world as a great training destination. Many people come for both. The truth is, there is no "typical" visitor to Lake Placid. Some people come to spend time in the wilderness, some come to be pampered in upscale resorts, some come to shop, some come to golf, some come to fish, some come for athletic events, and some come to sit on a secluded lakeside beach and do nothing at all.

Whatever the initial motivation is to come to Lake Placid, visitors most often discover that their expectations are far exceeded and they find themselves returning time and time again.

WHEN TO VISIT

There are two main tourist seasons in Lake Placid, summer and winter. Summer in the Adirondacks is hard to beat. Long, warm days with low humidity give way to cool, crisp nights. Stargazing is phenomenal and when the sun shines, a deep blue sky makes it near impossible to stay indoors. Winter draws snow lovers, skiers and those seeking a traditional holiday season of balsam, sleigh rides and gatherings around the fire. Fall and spring offer a less crowded alternative and unique outdoor events. The least popular months are April and November. Some establishments close during those months but for the most part, the town is open for business all year.

VISITOR INFORMATION CENTER

(49 Parkside Dr. Suite 2 ☎ 518.523.2445 ☗ lakeplacid.com) The Lake Placid CVB/Regional Office of Sustainable Tourism operates the Visitor Information Center in Lake Placid. The center is located on Parkside Drive near the beach on Mirror Lake.

GETTING TO LAKE PLACID

Lake Placid sits in the middle of the wilderness, but that doesn't mean it's not accessible. In the late 1800s the first steady stream of visitors arrived by railroad. It took days to reach the interior of the park, but that didn't stop people from coming. Today, visitors arrive by car, bus and plane. Roads are continually maintained and snow removal in the winter is some of the best in the country. Lake Placid is an easily accessible destination and its dependency on tourism ensures it will remain that way.

BY CAR

Arriving by car is the most popular way to reach Lake Placid. The drive from the Northway (I-87) along Route 73 is one of the most scenic in the park. It cuts through mountains, borders pristine lakes, and passes rock formations and waterfalls. Following are directions from several major metropolitan areas:

FROM NEW YORK CITY AND NEW JERSEY

Take the NY State Thruway (I-87) north to the Northway (exit 24 in Albany—to remain on I-87). Continue on I-87 to exit 30. Turn left on Route 9 (north) for two miles to Route 73. Continue on Route 73 for 28 miles into Lake Placid. The approximate drive time from New York City is 5 hours. The approximate drive time from Albany is 2.5 hours.

FROM BOSTON AND HARTFORD

Take the Massachusetts Turnpike (I-90) toward Albany. Take I-787 north to Cohoes. Take Route 7 west to I-87 north (Northway). Follow I-87 to exit 30. Turn left on Route 9 (north) for two miles to Route 73. Continue on Route 73 for 28 miles into Lake Placid. The approximate drive time from Boston is 5 hours.

FROM BUFFALO, ROCHESTER AND SYRACUSE

Take I-90 (NY State Thruway) east to exit 36 (Syracuse). Take I-81 north and continue to Watertown. Take Route 3 and follow it east to Saranac Lake. Take Route 86 east to Lake Placid. The approximate drive time from Buffalo is 5.5 hours. The approximate drive time from Rochester is 4.5 hours. The approximate drive time from Syracuse is 3.5 hours.

Area
Orientation

BY BUS

There is only one bus service provider to Lake Placid, Adirondack Trailways. Other bus services can connect to this service provider in major cities.

ADIRONDACK TRAILWAYS

(☎ 800.776.7548 ⌂ trailwaysny.com) Adirondack Trailways offers bus service between New York City, the Adirondacks, other locations in upstate New York and parts of Canada. There are several bus stations in the park, including **Lake Placid** *(2634 Main St.)*, **Saranac Lake** *(100 Main St.)*, **Keene Valley** *(1770 Route 73)* and **Lake George** *(35 Montcalm St.)*.

BY AIR

Lake Placid is a 2.5-hour drive from three major airports, Albany, New York; Montreal, Quebec; and Burlington, Vermont. Major airlines service all three airports and rental cars are available. There are also two regional airports, one in Lake Placid and the other in Saranac Lake that offer options for private and commercial air travel.

ALBANY INTERNATIONAL AIRPORT

(737 Albany-Shaker Rd, Albany ☎ 518.242.2200

✆ albanyairport.com, Airport Code: ALB) Albany International Airport is the most accessible major airport to Lake Placid. It is an easy drive up I-87 (Northway) into the park and there is normally little traffic.

MONTRÉAL–PIERRE ELLIOTT TRUDEAU INTERNATIONAL AIRPORT

(975, Roméo-Vachon Blvd. North Dorval, Quebec ☎ 514.394.7377

✆ admtl.com, Airport Code: YUL) Montréal–Pierre Elliott Trudeau International Airport is a good choice for international visitors, but for those coming from elsewhere in the United States it can be a more expensive option. The border crossing between Canada and the United States can also add time to the drive down.

BURLINGTON INTERNATIONAL AIRPORT

(1200 Airport Dr. South Burlington, VT ☎ 802.863.1889

✆ burlingtonintlairport.com, Airport Code: BTV) Burlington International Airport is a good option for those visiting Lake Placid. The only downside is that the ferry ride across Lake Champlain can add time to the trip.

ADIRONDACK REGIONAL AIRPORT

(96 Airport Rd. Saranac Lake ☎ 518.891.4600

☝ **saranaclake.com/airport, Airport Code: SLK)** The Adirondack Regional Airport is located 16 miles from Lake Placid in Lake Clear. It provides the only commercial airline service inside the park. Rental cars are available at the airport. Commercial service is somewhat limited, so make reservations early for peak season travel.

LAKE PLACID MUNICIPAL AIRPORT

(27 Airport Ln. Lake Placid ☎ 518.523.2473, Airport Code: LKP) The Lake Placid Municipal Airport is located just outside the village on Route 73. Air charter service is available from many airports; however, there are no commercial flights.

ADIRONDACK FLYING SERVICE

(27 Airport Ln. Lake Placid ☎ 518.523.2488

☝ **flyanywhere.com)** Adirondack Flying Service provides charter air service from almost any airport in the United States to the Lake Placid Municipal Airport.

BY TRAIN

There is no direct train service to Lake Placid. Visitors wishing to arrive by train will need to connect to a bus for the last 40 miles.

AMTRAK

(☎ 800.872.7245 ☝ amtrak.com) Amtrak provides service from multiple East Coast destinations. The closest rail station is in

Westport, New York, approximately 40 miles from Lake Placid. Bus service is available from Westport to Lake Placid.

GETTING AROUND

Lake Placid is pedestrian friendly. Most visitors staying right in the village choose to walk to the stores, restaurants, and venues located on Main Street and around Mirror Lake. However, reaching many of the Olympic attractions and activities surrounding the village requires a short car ride or transportation service.

PARKING

Parking is normally not a problem in Lake Placid, although during peak times or special events the public parking lots do fill up and street parking becomes scarce. There are several municipal parking lots located in the village. Each has its own restrictions for overnight parking, so visitors should read the signs posted carefully before leaving their vehicles. Most hotels have their own parking lots for guests.

There are two small lots on Main Street in the center of town, on the opposite side of the street from Mirror Lake. One is the Main Street Municipal lot and the other is the NBT parking lot across from the NBT Bank (this lot has an upper and lower section).

There is also a large lot near the **Olympic Center** across from the post office (on the bend in the road), and another municipal lot on Main Street between the Stewart's Shop and the **High Peaks Cyclery**.

Mirror Lake Drive has a municipal parking lot located next to the **Lake Placid Pub & Brewery**.

There is also electronic meter parking on the street. Overnight parking on Main Street is prohibited due to street cleaning— cars must be removed between the hours of 2 a.m. and 6 a.m. From November 1 through April 30, there is a parking ban on *all* village streets during the same hours.

LAKE PLACID XPRSS

(Main St. ☎ 518.523.2597) There is a free trolley service throughout Lake Placid called the Lake Placid XPRSS. The service runs all year although the schedule can change between seasons. The trolleys are wheelchair accessible and ADA compliant. Special service arrangements can be made by calling 24 hours in advance.

The trolley connects with the Mountain Valley Shuttle to Whiteface and Ausable Forks. Connections can be made at the **Lake Placid Olympic Center**.

Trolley schedules are available at the **Visitor Information Center** and throughout the village in brochure displays.

MOUNTAIN VALLEY SHUTTLE

(🖱 whiteface.com) The Mountain Valley Shuttle is a free shuttle between Lake Placid and the ski resort at Whiteface. The route begins at the **Mirror Lake Inn** (35-minute ride to the mountain) and stops in locations such as the **Crowne Plaza Resort, High Peaks Resort, Olympic Center** and **Art Devlin's Motel**. Skiers and non-skiers are welcome to ride the shuttle.

GROUND FORCE 1 LIMOUSINE & TRANSPORTATION

(2402 Main St. ☎ 518.523.0294) Ground Force 1 offers limousine, private SUV and private bus transportation services. They are available for events and individual transport. It is not uncommon to see their private bus driving around town—it's tempting to try to get a look inside at the plush accommodations. ($$)

TAXI SERVICES

Corrow's Adirondack Taxi *(59 McKinley St. ☎ 518.523.9091)* offers local taxi service in Lake Placid. They provide reliable service in and around the village. **Rick's Taxi** *(18 Spruce St. ☎ 518.523.4741)* also offers local taxi service in Lake Placid. They are privately owned and operated. *($)*

MEDICAL AND EMERGENCY SERVICES

Emergency police, fire and rescue services can be accessed by calling 911. The **Essex County Police Department** can be contacted for non-emergencies *(☎ 518.523.3306)*, and the **fire department** can be reached for non-emergencies *(☎ 518.523.3211)*.

The **Adirondack Medical Center** *(🖐 amccares.org)* has locations throughout the Adirondacks. It was founded in 1991, when the General Hospital of Saranac Lake and Placid Memorial Hospital in Lake Placid were consolidated. The primary hospital is located in Saranac Lake.

Olympic Venues

Only three locations in the world have hosted the Winter Olympics twice—Innsbruck, Austria; St. Moritz, Switzerland; and Lake Placid. This distinction will forever be a part of Lake Placid's resume. Some of the athletic venues in Lake Placid were used for both the 1932 and 1980 Winter Olympics, although many improvements were made during the 48 years in between.

Since 1980, the New York State Olympic Regional Development Authority (ORDA) has managed the Olympic facilities in Lake Placid including the operation of the **Whiteface Mountain** and **Gore Mountain** ski areas. ORDA has done a great job of maintaining the facilities while preserving the Olympic history. To this day, most of the Olympic venues are used year-round for training, competitions and as tourist attractions. ORDA hosts many national and international events, and brings millions of athletes and spectators to the village.

Visitors to Lake Placid are continually reminded of the village's athletic history. Most of the Olympic venues are open to the public and events are held throughout the year. Additional information about **ORDA** can be found online (🖱 *orda.org*).

OLYMPIC CENTER

The **Olympic Center** *(2634 Main St. ☎ 518.523.1655 🖱 whiteface. com)* is the dominant feature on Main Street. Nestled between the Lake Placid Conference Center and the Lake Placid High School, the Olympic Center was the site of both indoor and outdoor skating events in the 1932 and 1980 Olympics. The center now hosts numerous international figure skating competitions, hockey tournaments, and professional ice shows and is used by athletes from across the globe as a training center. The Olympic Center is also used as a base for the New York Islanders *(NHL)* preseason training camp and is home to the USA Hockey Women's National Team.

The large Olympic rings and the Olympic Center message board as you enter the historic facility are hard to miss. Admission into the center during non-event hours is free, and you can walk right into the original ice rink for the 1932 Olympics on the upper level as well as the Herb Brooks Arena. The Herb Brooks Arena was built for the 1980 Winter Olympics and is named after the coach of the U.S. Hockey Team who captured world attention in the famous Olympic victory over the Soviet Union known as "Miracle on Ice." Information on this game and other Olympic moments can be found on the lower level of the Olympic Center at the Olympic Museum. Guided tours of the facility are also available.

FREAKY FRIDAY - ICE SHOW

(Olympic Center) Visitors can watch up and coming Olympic skaters perform creative and often humorous ice routines. Presentations are judged on entertainment value rather than precision. Admission is free to the public.

SATURDAY NIGHT ICE SHOWS

(Olympic Center) Many of the world's best skaters train year-round in Lake Placid, and Saturday night ice shows in the summer are a tradition at the Olympic Center. Open most Saturdays, the ice shows provide opportunities for world-class skaters to perform in front of a live audience. Specific schedules and showtimes are available online.

LAKE PLACID FIGURE SKATING CHAMPIONSHIPS

(Olympic Center 🖱 lakeplacidskating.com) The Lake Placid Figure Skating Championships are held annually in June at the Olympic Center. The event is hosted by the Skating Club of Lake Placid and ORDA. It is sanctioned by **U.S. Figure Skating** *(🖱 usfsa.org)* and **Skate Canada** *(🖱 skatecanada.ca)*.

LAKE PLACID ICE DANCE CHAMPIONSHIPS

(Olympic Center 🖱 lakeplacidskating.com) The Lake Placid Ice Dance Championships are held annually in August at the Olympic Center. The event is hosted by the Skating Club of Lake Placid and ORDA. It is sanctioned by **U.S. Figure Skating** *(🖱 usfsa.org)* and **Skate Canada** *(🖱 skatecanada.ca)*.

CAN/AM HOCKEY TOURNAMENTS

(Olympic Center 🖱 canamhockey.com) For more than 20 years, CAN/AM Hockey has hosted youth hockey events in Lake Placid at the Olympic Center. Tournaments are now held throughout the year for both youth and adults. It is easy to tell when a youth tournament is taking place in town. Many young players wielding large hockey sticks can be seen walking up and down Main Street, lugging their gear bags between hotels and the Olympic Center. Visitors and those who wish to participate should consult the CAN/AM Hockey website for a schedule of events.

CANADIAN HOCKEY ENTERPRISES TOURNAMENTS

(Olympic Center 🖱 chehockey.com) Canadian Hockey Enterprises offers hockey tournaments for children and adults throughout the year at the Olympic Center. Lodging packages

Olympic Venues

that have accommodations within walking distance of the **Olympic Center** are offered to participants.

OLYMPIC JUMPING COMPLEX ✪ Must See!

It could be argued that a trip to Lake Placid isn't complete without a visit to the top of the **Olympic Ski Jump Complex** *(5486 Cascade Rd.* ☎ *518.523.2202* ◗ *whiteface.com)*. The process can be challenging to people with a fear of heights, but it is worth mustering up the courage. A chairlift takes visitors to the base of the 120-meter jump (on occasion, when the lift isn't running, visitors are instructed to drive to the base of the jump). If the structures didn't look daunting from afar, standing under them will surely stir the stomach butterflies.

The next part of the visit requires an elevator ride up the 120-meter structure. On the way to the elevator, secure your tourist status by posing for a photo on the Olympic podium; it may be a one-time opportunity to feel what it's like to stand for gold. The glass elevator provides an outstanding view of the mountains. Once at the top, there are indoor and outdoor viewing areas. A step out by the start bench leaves little to the imagination for what it's like to peer down the 120-meter track. Ski jumping competitions on television will never look the same!

The complex is located off Route 73 and is nearly impossible to miss given the magnitude of the jumps. Tickets are purchased at the stand in the parking lot. ($)

WET 'N WILD WEDNESDAYS

(Olympic Jumping Complex) Visitors can watch freestyle ski aerialists train on Wednesdays during July and August at the

Olympic Jumping Complex. Athletes practice and provide a demonstration of their skills as they perform flips and twists into a landing pool. Athletes are available after the demonstration to meet audience members and sign autographs. ($)

SOARING SATURDAYS

(Olympic Jumping Complex) Visitors to the Olympic Jumping Complex can watch some of the country's best ski jumpers, who live and train in Lake Placid, show off their talents on Saturdays during July and August. After flying off the 90-meter ski jump (nearly 27 stories high) at nearly 60 miles per hour, athletes land on green plastic mats to the cheers of the crowd below. The result is a jump the length of a football field. ($)

OTHER AREAS OF OLYMPIC INTEREST

Around town and nearby are several top attractions for visitors and Olympic sporting enthusiasts alike, including the **Olympic Sports Complex** and **Whiteface Mountain.**

OLYMPIC SPORTS COMPLEX

(220 Bob Run, Rte 73 ☎ 518.523.4436 🖳 whiteface.com) The Olympic Sports Complex is the site of the 1932 and 1980 bobsled track as well as the combination track for skeleton and luge. It is located five miles east of Lake Placid on Route 73 at Mt. Van Hoevenberg. A guided bus tour is available to view the facility, or else you can try out the bobsled firsthand with a half-mile ride on the Olympic Track. ($)

SHEFFIELD SPEED SKATING OVAL

(Main St. ☎ 518.523.1655 ⛄ orda.org) The Lake Placid Speed Skating Club hosts multiple speed skating races and time trials each year on the Olympic speed skating track. The oval is one of the few outdoor speed skating tracks remaining, and visitors can enjoy beautiful views of the ski jumps and surrounding mountains from the venue. Competitions are held on the same track where Eric Heiden won his famous Olympic medals, and the ice is open for public skating in the winter. See the "Winter Recreation" chapter for additional information.

WHITEFACE MOUNTAIN

(5021 Rte 86 Wilmington ☎ 518.946.2223 ⛄ whiteface.com) There are several ways to experience Whiteface Mountain. Winter visitors can ski more than 80 trails on Whiteface Mountain, where the Olympic downhill skiing events were held. Year-round visitors can take in the beauty of the Adirondacks via a scenic gondola ride. The summit of Whiteface Mountain can be hiked or accessed by the Whiteface Veterans Memorial Highway (toll road). See the "Summer Recreation" and "Winter Recreation" chapters for additional information.

Attractions

●

Lake Placid is a playground for children of all ages and tastes. The village itself offers shopping, beaches, many dining options, art galleries, performing arts, festivals, farmers markets, ice skating, spas, water sports, dog sledding and children's activities. The immediate area outside the Village of Lake Placid offers several world-class golf courses, historical landmarks, superb hiking, fishing, boating, rock climbing, ice climbing, camping, road biking, mountain biking, downhill skiing, cross-country skiing, snowshoeing, canoeing, whitewater rafting, kayaking, bird watching and horseback riding.

MUSEUMS AND LEARNING CENTERS

There is a lot more to Lake Placid than the Olympic venues. There are museums, historical sites, and learning centers in or near the village that are easily accessible to visitors. There are also local tour operators offering unique perspectives on the village—from the air, on the water, behind a team of horses or from a dog sled.

ADIRONDACK MUSEUM ✪ Must See!
(Rtes 28N and 30, Blue Mountain Lake ☎ 518.352.7311
🖱 **adkmuseum.org)** The Adirondack Museum is the premier museum in the park. Although it is located 63 miles from Lake Placid in Blue Mountain Lake, the drive there is highly scenic (passing by lakes and several small towns), and the museum itself is worth the drive.

The mission of the museum is to expand "public understanding of Adirondack history and the relationship between people and the Adirondack wilderness, fostering informed choices for the future." It is a noble cause, and for more than 50 years the museum has supported the mission.

The Adirondack Museum is known for its one-of-a-kind collection of Adirondack photographs, artifacts, fine art and archival materials, as well as its boat and wagon collection. There is a research library housed in the museum, and an education department offering courses, workshops, demonstrations, field trips and other special events.

With more than 20 exhibits, amazing gardens, historical buildings and wonderful views, it is easy to see why thousands of visitors enjoy the Adirondack Museum each year.

The museum is open seasonally, so visitors should call ahead or check the website for dates and times of operation. ($/$$)

JOHN BROWN'S FARM

(115 John Brown Rd. ☎ 518.523.3900) John Brown's Farm is a New York State historical site. The site offers visitors a glimpse into the life of John Brown, who was an abolitionist in the 1800s. Born in 1800, John Brown helped free slaves until his efforts finally cost him his life in 1859. His remains were buried at his farm in North Elba where his restored farmhouse and monument pay tribute to his life and efforts. The historical site is located behind the ski jump complex on John Brown Road. ($)

LAKE PLACID/NORTH ELBA MUSEUM

(242 Station St. ☎ 518.523.1608 ☗ lakeplacidhistory.com) The
Lake Placid/North Elba Museum is housed in a historical train
station in Lake Placid. More than 200 years are chronicled in
about a dozen exhibits. Some of the items on display include
photographs, agricultural equipment, musical instruments,
rocks and minerals. ($)

U.S. OLYMPIC TRAINING CENTER - LAKE PLACID

(196 Old Military Rd. ☎ 518.523.2600 ☗ teamusa.org) The
U.S. Olympic Training Center in Lake Placid is a training and
housing complex for athletes and is completely separate from
the Olympic Center. It was built to assist athletes in their
pursuit of Olympic sports. The training facility also supports
affiliated sports organizations including disabled sports organizations. Since 1982, the center has helped winter sports athletes
train in biathlon, bobsled, figure skating, luge, hockey, skiing,
and speed skating, and summer sports athletes train in boxing,
canoe and kayak, rowing, judo, synchronized swimming,
taekwondo, team handball, water polo and wrestling.

Parts of the training center are open to visitors, while the
housing facility provides private living quarters to athletes. The
housing facility consists of 96 private rooms and 11 common
area rooms. The adjoining athlete center contains a 20,000
square foot gymnasium where events are hosted. There is an
official **U.S. Olympic Spirit Store** in the lobby of the center.
This store is open to the public and is the only store in Lake
Placid that directly supports the U.S. athletes.

Visitors can tour parts of the facility and spectate during
competitions. It is not uncommon for visitors to be able to

walk right into international athletic competitions and grab a front row seat for free. A list of events can be found on the training center website.

LAKE PLACID WINTER OLYMPIC MUSEUM

(Olympic Center, 2634 Main St. ☎ 518.523.1655
🖱 whiteface.com) The Lake Placid Winter Olympic Museum is hidden in a back corner of the **Olympic Center**. It is worth the nominal entrance fee to view memorabilia from both the 1932 and 1980 Olympics, as well as treasures from other Winter Olympics. The museum is small (one room), but packed with interesting exhibits and videos. Visitors can enjoy displays of Olympic medals, Olympic torches, antique bobsleds, autographed hockey sticks, Team USA clothing, vintage Olympic gear, photographs and movie props from *Miracle*. There is also a dedicated exhibit for the 1980 U.S. Olympic hockey team with footage from the televised broadcast of their victory against the Soviet Union. ($)

PAUL SMITH'S COLLEGE

(Rte 86 and Rte 30 Paul Smiths ☎ 518.327.6227
🖱 paulsmiths.edu) Paul Smith's College is the only four-year private college located in Adirondack State Park. They are known as an innovator in hands-on learning. They offer degrees in disciplines such as culinary arts, hotel and restaurant hospitality, outdoor recreation, ecology, and natural resources. The beautiful lakefront campus is a nice place to visit and serves as a local venue for events. It is located 22 miles northwest of Lake Placid.

ROBERT LOUIS STEVENSON COTTAGE AND MUSEUM

(44 Stevenson Lake, Saranac Lake ☎ 518.891.1462

⬤ robertlouisstevensonmemorialcottage.org) The Robert Louis Stevenson Cottage and Museum is a rustic farmhouse where Robert Louis Stevenson (author of *Treasure Island*) lived after moving to Saranac Lake from England. The house is preserved in its original state and has the largest collection of Stevenson's personal items.

SARANAC LABORATORY MUSEUM

(89 Church Street, Ste 2, Saranac Lake ☎ 518.891.4606

⬤ historicsaranaclake.org) The Saranac Laboratory Museum was recently opened to the public to help visitors understand Saranac Lake's unique history and the work Dr. Edward Livingston Trudeau did with tuberculosis more than 100 years ago. The museum was Dr. Trudeau's original laboratory, which was the first one in the United States to research tuberculosis. The museum exhibits are run in partnership with the Trudeau Institute and the Adirondack Museum. The exhibit is open seasonally and any time of year by appointment. ($)

Attractions

THE WILD CENTER ✪ Must See!

(45 Museum Dr. Tupper Lake ☎ 518.359.7800

⬤ wildcenter.org) The Wild Center in Tupper Lake (about 30 miles from Lake Placid) is a great place to learn about outdoor life in the Adirondacks. The center sits on 31 acres, and has hands-on activities and live animals that are native to the area. The exhibits are interesting and well presented and there are plenty of nature guides available to help visitors explore. The museum has both indoor and outdoor exhibits, events and educational opportunities. The center's website also offers a self-guided driving tour from Lake Placid to The Wild Center that visitors can print out and follow to get the most out of their drive to the center. ($/$$)

TOURS

There are so many ways to experience Lake Placid and the surrounding area that it's difficult to know where to begin. Following are several tour options for getting acquainted with the region.

ADIRONDACK FLYING SERVICE

(27 Airport Ln. ☎ 518.523.2488 ⬤ flyanywhere.com) One of the most exhilarating ways to experience the beauty of Lake Placid and the Adirondacks is by taking a scenic flight. Seeing the Adirondacks from the air brings a completely new perspective on the vastness of the park and how unspoiled the wilderness is. It is also a great way to view the Olympic venues and become familiar with the village orientation.

Adirondack Flying Service offers scenic 20-minutes flights out of the **Lake Placid Municipal Airport**. Sights include the High Peaks, lakes and Olympic venues. Families with up to two adults and three children can fly together. ($$/$$$)

LAKE PLACID BOAT TOURS

(Lake Placid Marina ☎ 518.523.9704 ⬤ lakeplacidmarina.com) A well-rounded trip to Lake Placid can include a scenic boat ride on Lake Placid itself. There are many beautiful Adirondack camps on the lake and great views of the surrounding mountains.

Lake Placid Boat Tours takes visitors on an hour-long pontoon boat cruise on Lake Placid. The tour is narrated and guests learn about the estates that line the lakeshore, wildlife and **Whiteface Mountain**. A nice introduction to the lake and the Village of Lake Placid, this tour is wonderful for families and groups. Tours leave from the Lake Placid Marina. ($/$$)

ADIRONDACK EQUINE CENTER
(Rte 86 ☎ 518.834.9933
🖱 adirondackequinecenter.com/sleigh.html) It would be hard to find a more authentic winter tour in the Adirondacks than a horse drawn sleigh ride. Trotting over the river and through the woods with hot cocoa and a personal guide is a fun and exciting way to experience winter in the North Country.

The Adirondack Equine Center offers guided sleigh rides throughout the winter. They offer private tours during the day and also by lantern at night. The sleigh is comfortable in all types of weather, and blankets and hot cocoa are provided. Tours go through open fields and forest. Scenery includes the ski jumps, High Peaks, and Sentinel ranges. Reservations are required, and private rides and times are available. ($$)

HISTORIC WALKING TOURS
(89 Church St., Ste 2 Saranac Lake ☎ 518.891.4606
🖱 historicsaranaclake.org) Historic walking tours can be a great way to get an overview and background information about a town. They also give visitors the opportunity to ask questions about the history of the town or particular buildings.

Seasonal historic walking tours of downtown Saranac Lake are provided for a small fee by Historic Saranac Lake, a not-for-profit architectural preservation organization. Tours run until the beginning of October and are held on Tuesday mornings. Tours begin at the **Harrietstown Town Hall** and end at the **Saranac Laboratory Museum**. ($)

ARTS AND MUSIC

Lake Placid is very well rounded for its small size. The natural beauty of the Adirondacks has inspired artists in all disciplines for decades. While painters focused on capturing the landscape on canvas, the performing arts grew as more and more visitors came to vacation in the area. The result is a thriving culture of art, theatre and music in Lake Placid, born out of both local and international influences. There are many opportunities for visitors to enjoy musical and theatrical performances, admire local galleries, or partake in workshops to further their own skills.

ADIRONDACK ARTISTS GUILD
(52 Main St., Saranac Lake ☎ 518 891.2615 ☗ adirondackartistsguild.com) The Adirondack Artists Guild is a cooperative art gallery located in Saranac Lake. It offers local artists the opportunity to show and sell their work. The guild also features guest artists and sponsors cultural events.

ADIRONDACK CRAFT CENTER
(114 Saranac Ave. ☎ 518.523.2062) The Adirondack Craft Center presents crafts created by more than 300 local and national artists. Items offered include glass, furnishings, books, sculptures, pottery, jewelry, photography, food products and quilts. The center was established in the mid-1980s and is located on Saranac Avenue.

BLUSEED STUDIOS

**(24 Cedar St., Saranac Lake ☎ 518.891.3799
◍ bluseedstudios.org)** Bluseed Studios is a ceramic and print-making studio with a 2,000-square-foot performance and gallery space. The studio is housed in a historic warehouse in Saranac Lake. It was founded as a project space where artists would have the ability to share diversity with the community. The studio maintains a full schedule of exhibits and concerts on its website.

JAY CRAFT CENTER

(Rte 9, North Jay ☎ 518.946.7824) The Jay Craft Center, located in Jay (about 17 miles from Lake Placid), contains a working pottery studio and a local craft gallery. The center is housed in the historic Grange Hall in Jay, and visitors are welcome to browse the crafts displayed and visit the pottery studio.

LAKE PLACID CENTER FOR THE ARTS

(7 Algonquin Dr. ☎ 518.523.2512 ◍ lakeplacidarts.org) The Lake Placid Center for the Arts is a year-round art complex that was founded in 1972. Performing arts presentations at the center include theatre, dance, music, film and family presentations with well-known artists from around the country. Although the center is perhaps most recognized for its performing arts, it originally opened as an art school and to this day hosts a variety of visual art exhibits throughout the year. The center also offers workshops, special events and art shows. A calendar of events is maintained on their website.

LAKE PLACID INSTITUTE

(☎ 518.523.1312 🌢 lakeplacidinstitute.org) The Lake Placid Institute develops high-quality arts and humanity programs aimed at enhancing the cultural life of the Adirondack region. Some of their offerings include poetry contests, documentary film presentations, music seminars, roundtables and other events. Their offices are housed in the North Elba Town Hall, and they utilize a number of spaces in nearby venues for their performances and programs. Information on current events can be found on their website.

LAKE PLACID SINFONIETTA

(☎ 518.523.2051 🌢 lakeplacidsinfonietta.org) The Lake Placid Sinfonietta is a chamber orchestra that performs during July and August in various locations in Lake Placid and nearby venues. Performances are on Wednesdays and Sundays, and feature some of the best classical musicians from across the country. Performers come from university faculties and larger orchestras. The Sinfonietta website provides details for each performance and the summer schedule.

SONGS AT MIRROR LAKE MUSIC SERIES

(Mid's Park, Main St. 🌢 songsatmirrorlake.com) The Songs at Mirror Lake Music Series is a free seven-week concert series held at Mid's Park, located in the center of the Village on Main Street in Lake Placid. Concerts begin at the end of June and are held on Tuesday evenings. Performances include local and regional artists. Visitors are encouraged to bring lawn chairs and blankets to enjoy the music and expansive view of Mirror Lake. A listing of concerts can be found on the music series' website.

FAMILY FUN

There are countless family activities to take advantage of in Lake Placid. In addition to the opportunities offered in the great outdoors, there are several in-town attractions that cater specifically to children and families.

AVALANCHE ADVENTURES

(1991 Saranac Ave. ☎ 518.523.1195

⬤ avalancheadventures.com) Avalanche Adventures is a small theme park located a few minutes from Main Street on Saranac Avenue. They offer a mini golf course, EuroBungy, a cave maze, rock climbing wall and an arcade. The park is open all year. ($)

BOWLWINKLES

(2750 Main St. ☎ 518.523.7868 ⬤ bowlwinkles.net)
Bowlwinkles Family Entertainment Center is open all year on Main Street. They offer bowling, "cosmic rock" and bowling, an arcade and laser tag. There is also a bar and grill on site. It is a great place to turn the kids loose when they have extra energy and the weather isn't cooperating. ($)

MIRROR LAKE BEACH

(Parkside Dr. and Mirror Lake Dr.) Mirror Lake Beach is a public facility located at the bottom of Mirror Lake (near the **Lake Placid Toboggan Chute** and **Visitor Information Center**). There is a public changing facility with bathrooms. The beach offers nice swimming in the warmer months and is also the starting line for boat races and the swim leg of *Ironman USA*.

THE NORTH POLE

(324 Whiteface Memorial Hwy, Wilmington ☎ 518.946.2211
✆ northpoleny.com) Children of all ages can experience the
magic of Christmas at the historic North Pole, Home of
Santa's Workshop. The North Pole opened in 1949 and was a
pioneer in American theme parks. The park is tucked into the
side of **Whiteface Mountain** and features Christmas-themed
buildings such as Santa's House and the reindeer barn (with
real reindeer), shows, shops, and an operating post office where
visitors can get a North Pole postmark. ($$)

PIRATE'S COVE ADVENTURE GOLF

(1980 Saranac Ave. ☎ 518.523.5478) Pirate's Cove Adventure
Golf is a mini golf course located a few minutes from Main
Street on Saranac Avenue. The course is open regularly
between Memorial Day and Labor Day. Visitors wishing to play
outside those dates should call ahead for hours. ($)

FESTIVALS

Lake Placid is the perfect venue for festivals. The town embraces
events, and locals and visitors alike partake in them year-round.

Spring is the slowest time of year for festivals around Lake Plac-
id. The weather is the most unpredictable in the spring, as winter
struggles to let go and summer fights to take hold.

Summer is prime festival time in Lake Placid. The weather can
be perfect and the village is flooded with visitors.

Fall is also a great time for festivals in the Adirondacks. The sun seems to shine the most in the fall and the crisp invigorating air and splendid fall foliage beckon people to play outdoors.

Lake Placid not only embraces the cold weather of winter, but also celebrates it all season. As the temperature drops, people simply add layers and continue on their way. The holidays also trigger festivals in the Adirondacks. The high snowfall leaves everything blanketed in fresh white powder and seems to put everyone in a holiday mood.

FESTIVAL OF FOOD AND WINE

(Spring, Mirror Lake Inn, 77 Mirror Lake Drive ☎ 518.523.2544 ❂ mirrorlakeinn.com) Those looking for an upscale wine tasting event may enjoy the annual four-day Festival of Food and Wine hosted by the **Mirror Lake Inn**. The event takes place in April, and a variety of passes are available and include a combination of tastings, dinners and accommodations at the inn. Various winemakers and vineyards are presented at the festival, and meals are prepared by nationally recognized guest chefs. Please consult the Mirror Lake Inn website for details. ($$$)

LAKE PLACID FILM FORUM

(Summer ☎ 518.523.3456 ❂ lakeplacidfilmforum.com) The Lake Placid Film Forum is an annual four-day event held in June. The Adirondack Film Society hosts the forum and the location of activities varies from year to year. The event was created to inspire independent filmmakers and foster creativity among original and adapted screenplays. It is also intended to exhibit new, rare and classic films. Events include seminars, workshops, screenings, screenplay readings, master classes, an outdoor actor's roundtable and a 24-hour filmmaking competition for college film students. Please consult the forum website for event dates and locations. ($)

I LOVE BBQ FESTIVAL

(Summer, Sheffield Speed Skating Oval ☎ 518.637.1593 ⊌ ilbbqf.com) The annual I Love BBQ Festival is held on the **Sheffield Speed Skating Oval** over the fourth of July. For three days, more than 40 teams and junior competitors compete in multiple categories to raise money for the Shipman Youth Center. More than 8,000 visitors attend the festival yearly to enjoy excellent food, music and other festivities. In recent years, the Junior World BBQ Championship has been held at the festival for which winning team members share a $10,000 scholarship to **Paul Smith's College**, located near Lake Placid. ($)

JULY 4TH PARADE & CELEBRATION

(Summer, Main St. and Mirror Lake Beach ⊌ lakeplacid.com) Lake Placid's annual Fourth of July celebration includes a parade down Main Street in the afternoon and a fireworks display set to music on Mirror Lake. This celebration has a heartwarming and patriotic feel to it.

ARTWALK IN SARANAC LAKE

(June-September, Saranac Lake) Several towns in the Adirondacks offer ArtWalks in the summer. The closest ArtWalk to Lake Placid is held in Saranac Lake. The walks offer the opportunity for local artists to demonstrate their work during special evening hours.

For more than a decade, downtown Saranac Lake has hosted ArtWalks on the third Thursday of the month from June through September. Local artists display their work and provide demonstrations at downtown galleries and stores. Visitors are invited to browse the artwork and take advantage of the opportunity to speak with the artists. A special ArtWalk is also held on the first Thursday in December.

OLYMPIC CAR SHOW & PARADE

(Fall, Sheffield Speed Skating Oval ☎ 518.523.2633 lakeplacidskiclub.com) The annual Olympic Car Show & Parade is held in early September at the **Sheffield Speed Skating Oval**. The event is sponsored by the Lake Placid Ski Club and is a judged show featuring approximately 100 cars. Visitors can watch the parade of cars around Mirror Lake and then get a closer look when the cars are parked on the oval. The event is free to spectators.

FESTIVAL OF THE COLORS

(Fall, Springfield Rd., Wilmington ☎ 518.946.2255 whitefaceregion.com) The Festival of the Colors is an annual autumn tradition in Wilmington. The festival features arts and crafts, live entertainment, fresh produce, furniture, photography, baked goods and games. The event is hosted by the Whiteface Mountain Regional Visitors Bureau and is held in the ball field on Springfield Road.

OKTOBERFEST

(Fall, 5021 Rte 86, Wilmington ☎ 518.946.2223 whiteface.com) Visitors looking for a place to show off their lederhosen will enjoy the annual Oktoberfest held at the

Whiteface Ski Area. The celebration takes place over a fall weekend (usually the first weekend in October) and offers traditional German music, beer, food and dancing. Discounted gondola rides to the top of **Little Whiteface Mountain** are available for those wishing to soak in the fall foliage, while back at the base of the mountain there are craft vendors and rides. ($)

FLAMING LEAVES FESTIVAL

(Fall, Olympic Jumping Complex, 5486 Cascade Rd.
☎ **518.523.2202 ⬤ whiteface.com)** The Flaming Leaves celebration in October is a fall festival and ski jumping competition rolled into one. The annual event spans two days and includes bands, barbecue, games and craft vendors. Dates vary from year to year, so visitors should check the website for current-year dates. ($)

FIRST NIGHT - SARANAC LAKE

(Winter, Saranac Lake ⬤ firstnightsaranaclake.org) Saranac Lake sponsors a First Night New Year's Eve celebration in downtown Saranac Lake. Many merchants and venues participate in the event, and the all-volunteer board works throughout the year to plan a day and evening of music and theatrical performances, workshops and culinary delights. The purpose of the event is to bring the community together to celebrate the arts and the New Year. A schedule of events is available on the event website.

ADIRONDACK INTERNATIONAL MOUNTAINFEST

(Winter, Keene Valley ⬤ mountaineer.com) The Adirondack International Mountainfest is an annual festival in nearby

Keene Valley geared toward ice climbing and mountaineering. The festival is held in January and includes presentations, ice climbing classes, slide shows, group dinners, gear demos, safety clinics and snowshoe mountaineering. ($/$$)

BANFF MOUNTAIN FILM FESTIVAL
(Winter, 17 Algonquin Dr. ☎ 518.523.2512
☗ chestnutmtnproductions.com) The Banff Mountain Film Festival is a traveling outdoor adventure film event that visits Lake Placid in late January. The festival is short—only one evening—and features top mountain films on topics such as mountaineering, climbing, wildlife and mountain sports. ($)

WINTER CARNIVAL - SARANAC LAKE
(Winter, Saranac Lake ☗ saranaclake.com) Winter Carnival in Saranac Lake is an annual tradition dating back more than a century. For two weeks, locals and visitors alike, enjoy festivities throughout the village including parades, fireworks displays, sporting events, dinners and galas. The theme of the carnival changes every year and Saranac Lake local, Garry Trudeau, creator of the *Doonesbury* cartoon, designs a collectible carnival pin that is for sale throughout the season in local shops and at city hall. The centerpiece for the event is the ice castle erected each year in the waterfront park at Lake Flower. The event is held at the beginning of February, and a schedule of activities can be found on the Saranac Lake website.

SPARKLE VILLAGE ARTS AND CRAFTS SHOW
(Winter, 39 Main St., Saranac Lake ☎ 518.891.1990
☗ saranaclake.com) In early December, Saranac Lake shows off Sparkle Village with thousands of tiny white lights and sched-

Lodging

Lake Placid is by no means a bargain destination. That being said, good deals can be found in the off-season (spring and fall) and often hotels will run specials. Always ask when making a reservation if there are any packages or discounts available. Sometimes all it takes is an inquiry to receive a reduced rate. Another good practice is to check the website for an establishment of interest. Some hotels run Internet-only specials in hopes of driving traffic to their site.

There are many types of accommodations in and near the Village of Lake Placid. There are campgrounds, private inns, bed and breakfasts, motels, hotels and extravagant resorts. There are also private homes for rent. Some accommodations are seasonal, but many are available all year.

Before selecting accommodations, become familiar with the layout of the village. Visitors arriving for a specific event may want to select a hotel or inn within walking distance of the event, even if it means staying outside the village. Others may wish to have the convenience of walking to restaurants and shops instead of staying near an event venue.

As an example, visitors who come to Lake Placid in the winter to ski will oftentimes stay right in the village even though **Whiteface Mountain** is about seven miles away. Accommodations near the ski resort are often in high demand, but they also can be far away from the action of the village. The après ski time might therefore be more comfortable in the village atmosphere. On the other hand, visitors arriving for hockey camp at the **Olympic Center** can have the best of both worlds. They can select a hotel next door to the center, walk to their event and also walk to all the village amenities. Still some may enjoy camping or renting a private home on a lake or in a wilderness setting, versus staying in the village. In short, it pays to become acquainted with the town and surrounding area when selecting where to stay.

In general, Lake Placid is a dog-friendly town. Many establishments will accept dogs for an additional fee. This is not always advertised, so visitors traveling with a pet should inquire ahead of time.

LODGING ON MAIN STREET

Accommodations on Main Street are often the most sought after. They are within walking distance of shops and restaurants, and many local attractions.

ART DEVLIN'S OLYMPIC MOTOR INN

(2764 Main St. ☎ 518.523.3700 ⬛ artdevlins.com) Art Devlin's Olympic Motor Inn is named after Olympic ski jumper Art Devlin who was part of the U.S. Olympic team from 1940 to 1960. Devlin owned and operated the motel from 1953 until his son took it over in 1992. The motel originally offered just two motel rooms for rent, but has undergone many additions and extensive renovations over the past five decades. The current structure has European styling with stucco walls and wood ceilings. There are now 50 rooms for rent.

The motel is located just down the street from the main tourist area. There are many room types to choose from, including a spacious one-bedroom suite. Prices are reasonable for the good location and views. Light breakfast fare is included with a stay, and the motel is convenient to restaurants, shops and attractions. Rooms are clean and a rotating ongoing renovation plan keeps the facility up-to-date. The motel is dog friendly.

Visitors may notice that the Olympic rings appear on the motel sign, which is rare to see on a privately owned establishment. Since they were placed on the sign prior to 1962, when the International Olympic Committee trademarked the rings, they were allowed to remain under a grandfather clause. ($/$$)

BEST WESTERN ADIRONDACK INN

(2625 Main St. ☎ 518.523.2424 🖱 adirondack-inn.com) The family-owned chalet-style Adirondack Inn is centrally located across the street from the **Olympic Center** and steps away from the public beach on Mirror Lake. There are 49 nonsmoking rooms and suites. Rooms are clean and comfortable with cathedral ceilings and balconies on the second level. First-level rooms have patios. Rooms with two queen beds or one king bed are available. Connecting rooms are also offered.

The common areas include a comfortable seating area, breakfast room, and a small indoor pool and hot tub. There is also a sauna, fitness center and game room. Complimentary breakfast is included with all rooms as well as high-speed wireless Internet access. Ski and golf packages are available. Be sure to check the Internet for specials before making a reservation. ($$)

CROWNE PLAZA RESORT & GOLF CLUB

(101 Olympic Dr. ☎ 518.523.2556 🖱 lakeplacidcp.com) Undoubtedly, the Crowne Plaza has the best vantage point

of Lake Placid. Perched on a hill adjacent to the **Olympic Center**, the hotel overlooks Main Street with views of Mirror Lake and **Whiteface Mountain**. The rooms are a bit dated, and the steep walk up the hill to the resort can get old, but the common areas are well appointed and the indoor pool area is clean and attractive. Access to a private beach on Mirror Lake is included with each stay.

Other amenities include a fitness room, 30,000 square feet of event space, and wi-fi. The historic Lake Placid Club is also owned and operated by the Crowne Plaza Resort & Golf Club. The club has the only 45-hole golf course in the Adirondacks, and it is set against a backdrop of the High Peaks. Mackenzie's Restaurant is located in the hotel but the Lake Placid Club also has three additional restaurants in Lake Placid— the **Lake Placid Club Boathouse** (on Mirror Lake), the **Lake Placid Club Golf House** (located on the golf course) and **The Veranda** (located next to the hotel). ($$)

GOLDEN ARROW LAKESIDE RESORT

(2559 Main St. ☎ 518.523.3353 🌐 golden-arrow.com) Great views of Mirror Lake are the calling card of the Golden Arrow Lakeside Resort. The rooms are clean (although a little dated), the staff is friendly and the location on Main Street is hard to beat. The hotel has its own private beach, fitness room, and even an old but certainly useable racquetball court. The Golden Arrow Lakeside Resort is a landmark on Main Street, located on the bend in the road across from the large municipal parking lot. The hotel has its own parking and many fine amenities—a pleasant lakefront stay in a great location. ($$)

HIGH PEAKS RESORT ✪ Must See!

(2384 Saranac Ave. ☎ 518.523.4411 ☗ highpeaksresort.com)
The High Peaks Resort is made up of three separate facilities.
The Main Building, located on the corner of Main Street and
Saranac Avenue, offers mountain or courtyard views and king
and double-queen rooms. The Waterfront Building, located
around the corner on Mirror Lake Drive, fronts Mirror Lake
and offers direct lake access from every room. There's a collection of kayaks, rowboats and paddleboats for guests staying in
all locations. The third building, The Lakeview Motor Inn, sits
off Saranac Avenue and offers motel accommodations.

The location of the Main Building at the High Peaks Resort
has a long history of inn service. The original home was built
in 1876, and it became an inn in 1900—the Homestead. The
inn operated until 1977, when it was razed in order to build the
Hilton Lake Placid Resort. The hotel was converted in 2008 to
the High Peaks Resort.

The resort is well maintained and offers attentive service.
There are meeting facilities, a fitness center, indoor and
outdoor pools, and an Aveda spa and salon on site. There is
also a restaurant, **Dancing Bears**, which offers indoor and
second-level patio dining in warm weather (see the "Dining"
section). The patio is particularly nice. Visitors can enjoy views
of Mirror Lake and an open fire pit. The facility is pet friendly.
($$/$$$)

MOUNTAIN VIEW INN

(2548 Main St. ☎ 518.523.2439) The Mountain View Inn
offers comfortable, reasonably priced rooms overlooking Main
Street and Mirror Lake. The inn is conveniently located near

the **Olympic Center**, restaurants and shopping. The owners are friendly and go out of their way to make the inn inviting and guests feel welcome. Rooms are clean and tidy. Known to be a good value, the Mountain View Inn is a good choice for solid accommodations right in town. ($/$$)

NORTH WOODS INN

(2520 Main St. ☎ 518.523.1818 📱 northwoodsinn.com) The North Woods Inn is centrally located on Main Street among shops, restaurants and the movie theater. The hotel has a sidewalk café and two restaurants on site as well as a rooftop bar with great views of the town. The inn offers all suites for short and long-term stays. Many rooms have balconies. The North Woods Inn is a great base for tourists attending local events and is a top choice for visiting athletes. ($$)

ACCOMMODATIONS OFF MAIN STREET

There are many accommodations off Main Street that are still either in the village or convenient to village amenities. Most are within walking distance of shops and restaurants or just within a short drive.

COBBLE MOUNTAIN LODGE

(2983 Wilmington Rd. ☎ 518.523.2040
📱 **cobblemoountainlodge.com)** Cobble Mountain Lodge is located on Route 86 just outside of the main village (past the golf course) on the way to Wilmington. Their accommodations include cabins with kitchenettes and full-size cabins with one or two bedrooms. The cabins are cute and cozy, and offer

more privacy than a motel room. It is a nice place for families and visitors wanting to stay a little off Main Street. ($/$$)

COURTYARD BY MARRIOTT LAKE PLACID
(5920 Cascade Rd. ☎ 518.525.3752

📱 **courtyardlakeplacid.com)** A nice addition to the hotel offerings in Lake Placid, the Courtyard by Marriott Lake Placid is a nicely designed hotel just a short drive to the village attractions. The rooms are clean and spacious and the staff is welcoming. Rates are a bit lower than hotels that are located on Main Street. This hotel has an overall pleasant atmosphere for those wishing to stay a few minutes from the main drag. ($$)

LAKE PLACID LODGE
(144 Lodge Way ☎ 518.523.2700 📱 lakeplacidlodge.com) The Lake Placid Lodge is an exclusive lakefront hotel on Lake Placid. It offers luxurious accommodations with 13 waterfront rooms and 17 waterfront cabins. Each room has a wood burning fireplace and large windows. Rooms are very private and each is unique. There are also two cottages available for rent. The lodge is great for an upscale retreat destination or accommodations for a special getaway. ($$$+)

LAKE PLACID SUMMIT HOTEL RESORT & SUITES
(2375 Saranac Ave. ☎ 518.523.2587

📱 **lakeplacidsummithotel.com)** The Lake Placid Summit Hotel is located just around the corner from Main Street on Saranac Avenue. It may not be much to look at from the parking lot, but it offers views of Mirror Lake and easy access to shopping and restaurants. Rooms are decorated with standard hotel-style, no-frills furnishings. Double, queen, king and suite rooms are available. The facility also offers a 3,000-square-foot conference center, heated indoor pool, hot tub, high-speed Internet access, free parking and complimentary breakfast. Pets are allowed with some restrictions, and refrigerators are available upon request. Ski packages are also available. Service can be slow, but if location and reasonable prices are a top priority this may be a good choice. ($$)

STAGECOACH INN ✪ Must See!
(3 Stagecoach Way ☎ 518.523.9698
⬙ lakeplacidstagecoachinn.com) The Stagecoach Inn is one of those special places that lure visitors in from the street. The recently renovated historic inn is located minutes from the village, and offers an elegant and romantic ambiance. The rooms are beautifully decorated, and the staff is warm and helpful. The inn is a nice Adirondack experience that harkens to an era long ago. ($$)

THE MAPLE LEAF INN
(2234 Saranac Ave. ☎ 518.523.2471 ⬙ maple-leaf.net) The Maple Leaf Inn is a clean, friendly motel in close proximity to all the attractions. The owners are very helpful and pleasant, and the grounds are meticulously maintained. Accommodations are not fancy but they are comfortable, and there is parking on site. A variety of rooms are available, including two bedroom suites and efficiency kitchenettes. Rates are reasonable and the inn is a short but doable walk to Main Street. ($/$$)

THE MIRROR LAKE INN ✪ Must See!

(77 Mirror Lake Dr. ☎ 518.523.2544 ✆ mirrorlakeinn.com) The Mirror Lake Inn, a well-recognized landmark in the village, opened in the early 1920s as the Mir-a-Lac Inn. The inn overlooks Mirror Lake and offers an assortment of accommodations in several buildings. The Mirror Lake Inn has a history of sports connections. In 1932, the entire inn was rented by the Norwegian Olympic Team to use during the winter games. The inn also has its own outdoor ice skating rink and it was the first in the area to hold skating camps, which attracted many future world champions to its facilities.

The Mirror Lake Inn is located on Mirror Lake Drive, just steps from Main Street. Facilities include a private beach, two swimming pools (indoor and outdoor), tennis court, outdoor ice skating rink, hot tub and sauna.

Be sure to ask about the type of room you wish to rent, as they have many room categories and room styles. The most popular rooms are on the lakeshore. These rooms have the best views and extra amenities. Visitors looking to rent those should book well in advance. All rooms are pictured on the inn's website.

The staff is friendly, the common areas are clean and cozy, and the service is usually excellent. There are three restaurants on site. ($$$)

PARADOX LODGE RESTAURANT & INN

(2169 Saranac Ave. ☎ 518.523.9078 ✆ paradoxlodge.com) The Paradox Lodge is located less than a mile from Main Street in Paradox Bay on Lake Placid. The inn was originally built in 1899 and was renovated in 1998. Eight guest rooms, each individually decorated and furnished in Adirondack style, are available to rent in two separate buildings (Paradox Lodge and Cedar Lodge).

The common areas and front porch are plentifully furnished with rustic pieces and antiques. All rooms have a private bathroom, hair dryers and wi-fi. Select rooms have fireplaces and additional amenities. Accommodations are "not suitable for children" and no pets are allowed. Bicycle and ski storage is available. The inn is open year-round with the exception of April and November. Breakfast is served to all guests, and dinner is served to the public on a reservation basis. The restaurant was featured in Rachael Ray's *Tasty Travels* on the *Food Network*. ($$)

PLACID BAY INN

(2187 Saranac Ave. ☎ 518.523.2001 ⬤ placidbay.com) The Placid Bay Inn is a small, well-run inn directly on Lake Placid. They offer comfortable rooms, excellent service and clean accommodations. The inn is well located, is open all year and offers activities packages. ($$)

SWISS ACRES INN

(1970 Saranac Ave. ☎ 518.523.3040 ⬤ swissacres.com) The Swiss Acres Inn is located one mile from Main Street on Saranac Avenue, next to the Price Chopper shopping center. The establishment offers primarily motel rooms but also has four cabins for rent. They are known for having decent four-season accommodations at a good value. There are 54 rooms with a mix of double, queen and single beds. Dogs are allowed for an additional charge. Complimentary breakfast at the adjoining restaurant (Mr. P's) is included with their rooms.

There is a sports bar and heated outdoor pool on site. Golf packages are also available. ($/$$)

THE PINES INN

(2302 Saranac Ave. ☎ 518.523.9240

📍 thepinesoflakeplacid.com) The historic Pines Inn is located just a short walk from Main Street on Saranac Avenue. Built in 1907, the inn has undergone several renovations over the years. Its history includes visits from political officials such as Robert F. Kennedy and sports teams such as the Italian and Swiss bobsled teams. The Pines Inn has 35 rooms and is family owned and operated. There are rooms with double, queen and king beds and a few with micro-kitchenettes.

There is an indoor hot tub and wi-fi with a common computer in the main sitting area. There is also a restaurant on site called **Duncan's Grille**. ($$)

THE WHITEFACE LODGE

(7 Whiteface Inn Ln. ☎ 800.903.4045

📍 thewhitefacelodge.com) The Whiteface Lodge is a relatively new establishment located just outside the main tourist area of Lake Placid. It is a high-end resort with all the expected amenities and many additional perks such as an on-site movie theater, bowling alley, spa, game room and ice cream parlor. There is also twice-daily housekeeping.

From the moment visitors enter, they are engulfed in charming north woods decor. The elegant but rustic furnishings complement the beauty of the Adirondacks and the rooms are luxurious yet contemporary. There are three restaurants on site and a private canoe club on Lake Placid for guests. You pay for what you get at the Whiteface Lodge, since rooms are very pricey, but for those looking for luxury and ease, the establishment is difficult to beat. ($$$)

SURROUNDING AREA LODGING

There are many noteworthy accommodations outside the Village of Lake Placid that shouldn't be overlooked. Some offer rustic backcountry lodging for hikers and people pursuing any number of outdoor adventures. Others offer luxurious Great Camp atmospheres for wealthy travelers who wish to get away from it all in the comfort of an all-inclusive resort.

ADIRONDAK LOJ

(1002 Adirondak Loj Rd. ☎ 518.523.3441 🖱 adk.org) The Adirondak Loj at Heart Lake is owned and operated by the Adirondack Mountain Club. The original Adirondak Loj was founded by Henry Van Hoevenberg in 1890. Van Hoevenberg cut hiking trails from the lodge into the surrounding peaks, and encouraged early hikers to explore the area and learn about the wilderness. Many of the trails he cut are popular hiking routes today.

The current Adirondak Loj was built in 1927 and, like the original, is located on the shore of Heart Lake. It can accommodate 40 guests and offers private rooms, bunkrooms and a loft. Meals are made at the lodge and are served in the dining room. Accommodations are rustic and the atmosphere is relaxing.

The lodge is located eight miles south of Lake Placid and is open year-round. From Lake Placid, go three miles south on Route 73 toward Keene and Keene Valley. Turn right on Adirondak Loj Road at the High Peaks Trailhead sign. Continue five miles to the lodge. ($/$$)

GRACE CAMP AND CAMP PEGGY O'BRIEN

(☎ 518.523.3441 📞 adk.org) The Adirondack Mountain Club also offers year-round cabin rentals deep in the Johns Brook Valley. Grace Camp and Camp Peggy O'Brien are only accessible by hiking trail. Lean-tos are also available. The cabins are located a short distance from Johns Brook Lodge and are a great jumping off point for hikes in the Great Range. Cross-country skiing and snowshoeing are also good in the valley. Grace Camp can accommodate six people and Camp Peggy O'Brien can accommodate twelve.

From Lake Placid, follow Route 73 south to Keene Valley. At the High Peaks Trailhead sign next to the Ausable Inn, turn right onto Adirondack Street. After 0.6 miles, the road turns right and crosses Johns Brook. Follow the signs uphill to the Garden. The paved road will end at the approach to the Garden Parking Area. Parking is limited and will cost a small fee. It is a three- to-four-mile hike to the cabins. Visitors should make a reservation ahead of time ($/$$).

JOHNS BROOK LODGE

(☎ 518.523.3441 📞 adk.org) Johns Brook Lodge offers non-winterized hike-in accommodations for 28 guests. The lodge (also called JBL) is owned and operated by the Adirondack Mountain Club and is located in the heart of the High Peaks. The hike from the Garden Parking Area is 3.5 miles. Full-course meals are served in the summer time but the lodge is also open on a minimal basis during the spring and fall (guests can cook for themselves in the shoulder season on a large propane stove). Rustic accommodations include two family rooms and coed bunkrooms. Many great hikes are accessible from the lodge.

From Lake Placid, follow Route 73 south to Keene Valley. At the High Peaks Trailhead sign next to the Ausable Inn, turn right onto Adirondack Street. After 0.6 miles, the road turns right and crosses Johns Brook. Follow the signs uphill to the Garden. The paved road will end at the approach to the Garden Parking Area. Parking is limited and will cost a small fee. It is a 3.5-mile hike to the lodge. Visitors should make a reservation ahead of time. ($/$$)

SOUTH MEADOW FARM LODGE ✪ Must See!
(67 Sugarworks Way ☎ 518.523.9369 ♦ southmeadow.com)
South Meadows Farm is a quiet bed and breakfast located four miles outside the main tourist area of the Village of Lake Placid on Route 73. They offer seven well-appointed rooms, private bathrooms and a lot of privacy. The owners are wonderful hosts and clearly go out of their way to make their home comfortable to visitors and to accommodate their needs. A nice choice for travelers wishing to stay in a private setting close to town. A small sugarworks store selling maple syrup, gifts and other food items is also on site. ($$)

THE POINT
(Saranac Lake ☎ 518.891.5674 ♦ thepointresort.com) The Point is an exclusive, all-inclusive luxury resort on Upper Saranac Lake. Its exact location remains undisclosed except to paying guests and local residents. The Point refers to itself as a "vibrant and exclusive house party, an elegant hideaway,

the essence of rustic splendor, luxury and whimsy amid Adirondack Mountain wilderness."

The setting, service, staff and accommodations are known to be some of the best in the world. The price tag is out of reach for many, but those wanting to celebrate a special occasion or be pampered in a pristine setting may find it to be paradise. ($$$+)

CAMPING

Lake Placid is the quintessential area for camping. Birch and pine forests, cool glacial lakes, low humidity, endless outdoor activities, and great "sleeping" weather in the summer all add up to the perfect location for a camping vacation. Camping is always in style in the Adirondacks, and people dressed in fleece, wearing hats, and smelling like campfire just adds to the Adirondack ambiance around town.

There are several excellent camping options near Lake Placid. Many are established campgrounds that have easy access and are family and pet-oriented, while others are remote backcountry sites that offer hike-in or boat-in access only.

Many campsites (especially to the west of Lake Placid) are located on the shore of beautiful lakes and offer stunning waterfront views and superb fishing and paddling. Campsites in the High Peaks are often situation near popular trailheads and position campers to take advantage of the countless hiking trails in the area.

Some campgrounds are privately run and others are operated by the State of New York. Most are seasonal, although backcountry sites can be accessible all year. Campsites are in high demand in the summer months, so it's best to plan ahead and make a reservation during that time. Most campgrounds offer sites on a reservation-only basis.

BUCK POND

(1339 Country Rte 60, Onchiota ☎ 518.891.3449) Buck Pond is a beautiful waterfront campground operated by New York State. It offers stunning lake and mountain views, and has secluded campsites and plentiful water access. It is located on the western shore of Buck Pond, a 130-acre pond near Lake Kushaqua and Rainbow Lake. There are 116 campsites. Some of the amenities offered at the campground include hot showers, flush toilets, a bathing beach, walking trails, boat launch, car top boat launch, canoe rentals, bathhouse and trailer dump station. Everything from tents to 30-foot RVs are welcome. There are plenty of opportunities for canoeing, boating, fishing, biking and hiking. ($)

From Lake Placid, take Route 86 through Saranac Lake to Gabriels. In Gabriels, turn right on Franklin Country Road 60 (Rainbow Lake Road) toward Rainbow Lake. Buck Pond is six miles up (stay right at the sharp bend in the road by the camp store).

FISH CREEK POND STATE CAMPGROUND

(4523 State Rte 30, Saranac Lake ☎ 518.891.4560) Another stunning campground operated by New York State, Fish Creek Pond State Campground offers waterfront sites on Fish Creek. There is a natural sandy shoreline and most sites have water access. Several beautiful rivers and lakes are accessible to motorized and nonmotorized boats.

There are 355 sites that can accommodate tents and RVs up to 40 feet. The campground offers bathhouses with hot showers (coin operated), flush toilets, a trailer dumping station, boat launch, hiking trails, boat rentals, volleyball and basketball areas, picnic area and beach playground.

From Lake Placid, take Route 86 north through Saranac Lake to Route 186 west (turn left at the flashing light). Continue on Route 186 west and stay straight on Route 30 south. Continue nine miles to Fish Creek Pond (on the right side of the road). ($)

MEADOWBROOK

(1174 Rte 86, Ray Brook ☎ 518.891.4351) Meadowbrook is a great bargain for campers wanting to stay near town. Located in Ray Brook, the campground is only four miles from the center of Lake Placid. Meadowbrook is situated near numerous hiking trails for hikers of all abilities. There are 62 campsites, hot showers, flush toilets, a trailer dumping station and a recycle center. There is also a pavilion that can be rented for overnight guests or day use.

From Lake Placid, follow Route 86 west for four miles. Meadowbrook is located on the left side of the road in Ray Brook. ($)

NORTH POLE CAMPGROUND AND INN

(5644 NYS Rte 86, Wilmington ☎ 518.946.7733 ⬤ northpoleresorts.com) The North Pole Campground and Inn is a family-oriented, 120-acre resort near **Whiteface Mountain**. They offer private tent sites, 4-way hookups, camping cabins and cottages. Some sites are located on the

Ausable River. Some of the amenities include two outdoor pools, picnic area, boat rentals, fireplaces, game room and high-speed Internet. ($)

ROLLINS POND

(4523 State Rte 30, Saranac Lake ☎ 518.891.3239) Rollins Pond is a great place for paddlers and anglers to camp. The campground is located on the east side of Rollins Pond, a 44-acre pond. It is run by the State of New York, and there is a livery at the boat launch where visitors can rent kayaks, canoes, paddleboats or rowboats. Whey Pond, located adjacent to the boat launch is stocked with trout. There are 287 campsites. Tent sites and sites that can accommodate RVs up to 40 feet are available. Amenities include flush toilets, hot showers, a trailer dumping station, a boat launch for small boats, and hiking trails.

From Lake Placid, take Route 86 north through Saranac Lake. Turn left on Route 186 west (at the flashing light) and stay straight on Route 30. Drive nine miles to Fish Creek Pond Campground. Access to the Rollins Pond campground is through site number 135 in the Fish Creek Pond Campground. ($)

WHITEFACE MOUNTAIN KOA CAMPGROUND

(77 Fox Farm Rd., Wilmington ☎ 518.946.7878
🖱 koacampground.com) The KOA Campground near Whiteface is set in a lovely forest in the shadow of **Whiteface Mountain**. About a mile from the ski area, the campground is conveniently located to the Ausable River and the Wilmington Flume (waterfall). The campground is set on 70 acres and offers pull-thru sites, a "Kamping Kabin Village," log cabins and

cottages. There is also a heated pool, tennis, miniature golf, a playground, a game room and canoe rentals. The campground also has wi-fi. Reservations are required. Pets are allowed with some restrictions. ($/$$)

WILDERNESS CAMPGROUND AT HEART LAKE

(Adirondak Loj Rd. ☎ 518.523.3441 🖰 adk.org) The Wilderness Campground is operated by the Adirondack Mountain Club. It is located on Heart Lake, adjacent to the Adirondak Loj. The campground offers tent sites, lean-tos and canvas cabins (walled tents on wooden platforms). Tent sites and lean-tos hold up to six people.

The campground is located eight miles south of Lake Placid. From Lake Placid, go three miles south on Route 73 toward Keene and Keene Valley. Turn right on Adirondak Loj Road at the High Peaks Trailhead sign. Continue five miles to the campground. ($$)

WILMINGTON NOTCH CAMPGROUND

(4953 NYS Rte 86, Wilmington ☎ 518.897.1309) Wilmington Notch Campground is located eight miles from Lake Placid beside the Ausable River. The campground is located in a pine grove near the base of Whiteface Mountain. Activities include fishing and biking. Facilities include a comfort station, trailer dump station, recycle center, picnic tables, hot showers and flush toilets. There are 54 campsites. From Lake Placid, take Route 86 toward Wilmington. Drive eight miles to the campground. ($)

SARANAC LAKE ISLANDS

(4468 State Rte 3, Saranac Lake ☎ 518.897.1309) There are 87 beautiful, primitive, water access only campsites located on Middle and Lower Saranac Lakes. Camping permits are required for all sites. Parking is at the State Bridge Boat Launch on Route 3. Miles of boating and access to four lakes and excellent fishing make these popular camping destinations. ($)

RENTAL HOMES/CAMPS

Vacation homeowners in Lake Placid often open their doors to renters. Single-family homes, no matter what size, are often called "camps." Camps can be located on one of the many lakes or rivers, in the wilderness, or right in town.

The rental market is handled slightly differently in the Adirondacks than it is in other tourist areas. Instead of a handful of large real estate rental companies handling hundreds of rental homes, as often found in East Coast beach communities, a large percentage of homeowners handle their own rentals. The houses are most often advertised through a website—**Adirondack By Owner** (❂ *adkbyowner.com)*—but some use other websites or local advertisements to attract renters. Visitors can browse homes for rent, see an availability calendar for each home and find contact information for the homeowner to ask questions.

Some homeowners rent their properties through traditional real estate offices such as **Adirondack Associates Real Estate** *(2241 Saranac Ave.* ☎ *518.523.8884)*, **Adirondack Premier Properties, Inc.** *(2429 Main St.* ☎ *518.523.3333)*, **Century 21 High Peaks** *(2210 Saranac Ave.* ☎ *518.523.2547)*, and **Merrill L. Thomas, Inc.** *(2469 Main St* ☎ *518.523.2519)*.

Dining

Eating can be a big part of vacation. Whether a day in the great outdoors gets the appetite going, or an exciting day of sightseeing ends with the perfect meal, visitors find many restaurant options in Lake Placid to suit a variety of tastes. Whether a good barbeque sandwich with a locally brewed beer hits the spot, or a savory sea bass paired with a wonderful wine is more appealing, in most cases the right meal is just around the corner.

One word of caution—many establishments charge for soda refills. To avoid a surprise when the check comes, ask the server beforehand if refills are included.

MAIN STREET RESTAURANTS

Main Street is lined with multiple restaurant choices. It's hard to throw a stone without hitting a good place to dine. Many restaurants face Mirror Lake and many more have fireplaces or wood stoves that help make a cozy Adirondack atmosphere.

ASHLEY'S CAFÉ

(2726 Main St. ☎ 518.523.2540) Ashley's Café is located on Main Street, between the Olympic Center and the Route 73 traffic light. The owners run the restaurant and serve breakfast and lunch. Ashley's Café is known for their friendly service, clean facilities and fresh food. The menu includes many traditional breakfast and lunch items and all are done well. The pancakes are a favorite among patrons. Ashley's Café offers a friendly, inviting atmosphere and a convenient location. Reservations accepted. ($/$$)

BAZZI'S PIZZERIA

(2356 Main St. ☎ 518.523.9056) Bazzi's Pizzeria serves traditional-style New York pizza by the pie or by the slice. They offer dine-in, carry out and delivery. There are a few outdoor seats, and visitors sitting outside can bring their dogs. ($/$$)

BROWN DOG CAFÉ & WINE BAR ✪ Must See!

(2409 Main St. ☎ 518.523.3036) The Brown Dog Café & Wine Bar is a favorite with local residents and visitors. The food and the wine are excellent. The café also offers a prime view of Mirror Lake. At lunch they offer fresh, delicious designer sandwiches, and dinner has a more upscale menu (filet, crab cakes, duck, etc.). It's a good choice for wine enthusiasts and those in the mood for a little something different. ($$/$$$)

COFF E BEAN INTERNET CAFE

(Alpine Mall, 2527 Main St. ☎ 518.523.3228) The Coff E Bean is a coffee bar located in the Alpine Mall on Main Street. They offer a wide selection of drinks, and also serve breakfast and lunch. They are small but have a great view of Mirror Lake and a relaxing, friendly atmosphere. ($/$$)

DANCING BEARS

(High Peaks Resort, 2384 Saranac Ave. ☎ 518.523.4411 🖱 highpeaksresort.com) The Dancing Bears has a "primo" location on the corner of Main Street and Saranac Avenue and features two-story rounded windows from which to take in the street scene. It is hard to decide between watching the people outside or watching the large-screen TVs that surround the bar area.

The restaurant is clean and spacious, and is decorated with local sports memorabilia. The menu is mainly pub food and individual pizzas, but it is well prepared. Their signature "Mega-Freeze Polar Beers" are poured through taps encased in ice, resulting in super-cold drafts. The prices can't be beat on beer, and they offer a nice selection of labels. Whether you stroll in from shopping, skiing or a day on the water, the atmosphere is inviting and comfortable. It's a good place to meet friendly people on vacation from around the country, since it is part of the **High Peaks Resort**. ($$)

GENERATIONS RESTAURANT

(Golden Arrow Resort, 2559 Main St. ☎ 518.523.3353
☗ golden-arrow.com) Generations Restaurant is part of the **Golden Arrow Lakeside Resort**. It is open for breakfast, lunch and dinner and features locally grown and raised foods. A cozy bar with booths is located to the left as you enter the front door and the main dining area is to the right. There is also a seasonal deck. The menu is large and diverse. Breakfast offerings include omelets, frittata, pancakes, French toast and oatmeal. Lunch includes everything from sandwiches, burgers and pasta to seafood dishes. Dinner provides a choice of steak, pasta, seafood and a few Asian dishes. Reservations are accepted for parties of six or more. ($$)

GREAT ADIRONDACK STEAK & SEAFOOD COMPANY

(Great Adirondack Brewing Company, 2442 Main St.
☎ 518.523.1629 ☗ greatadirondacksteakandseafood.com) It is difficult for visitors in Lake Placid to miss seeing the Great Adirondack Steak and Seafood restaurant and the Great Adirondack Brewing Company. Located prominently on Main

Street, across from Mid's Park and Mirror Lake, the restaurant offers indoor seating and a large, inviting patio trimmed in flowers, market umbrellas and a wood burning fireplace.

The restaurant houses its own brewery out back and both are family owned and operated. The restaurant serves breakfast, lunch and dinner, and is open 365 days a year. Breakfast includes traditional items such as a variety of egg dishes, French toast and pancakes. Lunch includes chowders, burgers, salads and sandwiches. Dinner offers a large menu of starters, salads, seafood, steaks and pasta, to name a few. There are a number of beers on tap from the brewhouse, and the menu changes seasonally. ($$)

MR. MIKE'S

(332 Main St. ☎ 518.523.9770) Mr. Mike's is a good place to grab a pizza or call for delivery. They are an established restaurant on Main Street and can accommodate groups. The pizza is reliable and reasonably priced. A solid choice when the stomach is set on pizza. ($/$$)

NICOLA'S RESTAURANT COMPLEX

(211 Main St. ☎ 518.523.5853 🖋 nicolasandgrill211.com) Nicola's restaurant complex is located across from the **Olympic Center** on Main Street. There are two restaurants housed there, **Nicola's On Main** and **Grill 211**. Both are owned and operated by the same proprietor and they share one entrance.

Nicola's serves mostly Italian food such as pasta and pizza. Grill 211 offers mainly steaks and seafood. The building is inviting on the outside and centrally located. The atmosphere inside is spacious but not particularly cozy, due in part to the high ceilings and open floor plan. The food is tasty and the service is adequate. The wood-fired pizzas at Nicola's are a popular menu item, with their thin, crunchy crust. The desserts are also worth trying for visitors not counting calories. ($$)

SIMPLY GOURMET/BIG MOUNTAIN DELI & CRÊPERIE
⊗ Must See!

**(1983 Saranac Ave. & 2475 Main St. ☎ 518.523.3111
📱 simplygourmetlakeplacid.com)** Simply Gourmet and the Big Mountain Deli & Crêperie are operated in two locations in Lake Placid. The original (Simply Gourmet) location on Saranac Avenue is where their signature 46 sandwiches named for the 46 highest peaks in the Adirondacks were born. All are unique, delicious, customizable and served on fresh-baked bread. This location also offers a small market, baked goods (including fresh half-pound cookies) and a deli featuring fresh meat, cheese and seafood. Breakfast and lunch are made to order (with a large menu and daily specials) and take-out "cabin" dinners are also available. Order your food in the back and pay up front.

The Main Street location (Big Mountain Deli & Crêperie) serves breakfast, lunch (including the 46 sandwiches), dinner and a variety of sweet crepes. ($/$$)

SOULSHINE BAGELS ⊗ Must See!
(2526 Main St. ☎ 518.523.9772) Soulshine Bagels has become somewhat of a breakfast institution in Lake Placid. During big events, such as **Ironman USA**, the line can stretch out the door onto the street. The food is worth the wait, as the assortment of bagels including flavors such as graham cracker and

sunflower seed are made fresh and made well. Soulshine offers a nice assortment of sandwiches and cream cheese, and good quality coffee. ($)

RESTAURANTS OFF MAIN STREET

Visitors don't have to venture far off Main Street to enjoy additional good restaurant options. Many are still within walking distance to Main Street or else a short drive away.

ARTISANS - LAKE PLACID LODGE

(144 Lodge Way ☎ 518.523.2700 🖊 lakeplacidlodge.com)
Visitors seeking an idyllic lakefront setting may enjoy the fine dining offered at Artisans at the **Lake Placid Lodge**. Although the menu is somewhat limited, the setting, service and attention to detail can be worth the upscale price tag. For a celebration or a relaxing evening on a summer night, this is a nice choice. Reservations are advised. ($$$)

CAFFÉ RUSTICA ⊗ Must See!

(1936 Saranac Ave. ☎ 518.523.7511 🖊 cafferustica.com) Caffé Rustica offers quality Mediterranean-style food and creative specials. Located in the Price Chopper shopping center on Route 86, this little gem is small, friendly and consistent. The menu features wood fired pizzas, interesting pastas, salads and an extensive wine list. It is obvious that much thought goes into the development of the daily specials which are creative and more often than not, simply delicious. The owner and staff are friendly, social, and add to the casual but tasteful atmosphere. No reservations are accepted, so be prepared to wait during peak times. A seat at the bar can be surprisingly relaxing and also entertaining, as the kitchen is in open view to patrons. ($$)

CARIBBEAN COWBOY ✪ Must See!

(2126 Saranac Ave. ☎ 518.523.3836) Tucked away behind the **Sourdough Bakery**, the Caribbean Cowboy is a gem that is easily missed. They don't seem to advertise much, but regardless, they have a steady flow of both local and visiting patrons. The food is upscale Mexican, or "Caribbean," as they call it, with many seafood dishes and scrumptious specials. The price is higher that most Mexican restaurants and can be off-putting given the casual and somewhat funky atmosphere.

The preparation and presentation are excellent, with unique and flavorful combinations (the jerk chicken, fritters and spring rolls are favorites). The bar is well stocked and employs skilled bartenders—their Painkillers and Mango Margaritas are particularly tasty. The restaurant is located on the left side of Saranac Avenue as you drive west away from Mirror Lake. There is a large sign on the road, although it is still easy to miss. The restaurant is not visible from the street and is located in the back of the building by the parking lot. The Caribbean Cowboy is open year-round but is closed at least one day a week. ($$)

CHAIR 6 ✪ Must See!

(5993 Sentinel Rd. ☎ 518.523.3630 ⬤ chair6.com) Chair 6, named after the first ski lift chair to summit Whiteface Mountain, has made a name for itself by using high-quality organic ingredients and creating its menu items from scratch. The restaurant is small and quaint, located in a rustic white house just off the beaten path on Route 73. They serve breakfast, lunch and dinner, and offer take-out meals and homemade baked goods.

Arriving at the restaurant for breakfast or lunch, visitors feel like they are going to a friend's house for a casual meal. Selections include traditional breakfast items and sandwiches but many offer something a little special, such as a red pepper spread or balsamic dressing.

At dinnertime, the tiny dining area is transformed into an elegant, candlelit eating space with seasonal table arrangements and white tablecloths. Guests can expect friendly yet highly professional service and a lot of individual attention. The menu is a diverse offering of carefully planned fare featuring seafood, vegetarian and meat entrees accompanied by unique vegetable purees and other specialty side dishes. Whether the selection is filet, sea bass or the pasta of the day, guests will enjoy a beautifully presented and equally delicious meal, and oftentimes a personal visit from the chef.

Seating is limited, so reservations are recommended. From Main Street, head east to the Route 73 junction. Turn right at the traffic light and continue until you see the Chair 6 sign on the right. ($$)

DOWNHILL GRILL

(6143 Sentinel Rd. ☎ 518.523.9510) The Downhill Grill offers a wide menu that includes Mexican food, steak, seafood, salads and sandwiches. It is a good choice for groups with a variety of tastes and is often less crowded than some of the restaurants on Main Street during peak season. From Main Street, head east to the Route 73 junction. Turn right at the traffic light.

The Downhill Grill is appropriately located near the bottom of the hill on the right. ($/$$)

LAKE PLACID CLUB GOLF HOUSE

(88 Morningside Dr. ☎ 518.523.2556 🖱 lakeplacidcp.com) The Lake Placid Club Golf House offers one of the best views of the High Peaks and Olympic Ski Jumps in Lake Placid. The restaurant is open for lunch during the summer and shoulder seasons only (the exact dates vary depending on the weather and volume of business).

The restaurant itself is a beautiful open-beam room with a large stone fireplace, antler chandeliers and picture windows opening to a comfortable covered patio. The menu is somewhat limited, but features sandwiches, burgers and salads all creatively named with a golf theme. Traditional menu items such as the "The PGA Burger" and the "B.L. Tee" are complemented by a few well-thought-out specialties, such as the "Bogey" (sliced turkey breast with cranberry and brie) and the "Caesar in the Rough" (Caesar salad with herb crostini and chicken). A small selection of beer and wine is available as well as nonalcoholic drinks. The facility is owned by the **Crowne Plaza Resort** and is available for rent for weddings and corporate events. ($/$$)

LAKE PLACID PUB & BREWERY ✪ Must See!

(813 Mirror Lake Dr. ☎ 518.523.3813 🖱 ubuale.com) A few steps off the main drag sits a converted church housing the Lake Placid Pub & Brewery. As you enter, the original bar, P.J. O'Neill's, is located to the left. A stairway leading to the main dining room, a second bar and outdoor deck is located straight ahead. Most tourists prefer to go upstairs, where a stone fireplace warms the room in winter.

During the summer and ski season, there is usually a wait for a table. Come relax, have a beer and plan to wait. It will also take a while for food to arrive, as the kitchen is located downstairs and servers must carry food up. The beer is excellent, with seasonal rotating brews and a solid menu of year-round selections. The signature beer, Ubu Ale, is well known throughout the region and has even been served at the White House. The menu contains a variety of pub fare. Local favorites include the fish and chips, and the pub burrito. ($/$$)

LISA G'S

(6125 Sentinel Rd. ☎ 518.523.2093) Don't let the plain exterior on Sentinel Road be a deterrent to trying a meal at Lisa G's. The interior is clean and comfortable, and there is a lovely deck in back near the river. The menu is full of interesting surprises such as edamame dip, mashed potato pizza, and the Moroccan burrito. There are also traditional selections such as burgers, salads, pasta and many vegetarian dishes. The service is terrific and portions are very generous. There is an inviting lounge in the bar area with a big-screen television, but the television isn't on all the time, providing a nice relaxing place for cocktails when the weather isn't nice. From Main Street, head east to the Route 73 junction. Turn right at the traffic light. Lisa G's is located at the bottom of the hill on the right. ($/$$)

SARANAC SOURDOUGH

(2126 Saranac Ave. ☎ 518.523.4897) Saranac Sourdough is a casual breakfast, lunch and dinner shop selling sandwiches, salads, specialty meats and cheeses. They are located close to

Main Street on Saranac Avenue. The store began as a seasonal bread company in Saranac Lake but has been in its Lake Placid location since 1998. Everything is made in-house and they use fresh, seasonal and whenever possible, organic ingredients. They also make homemade soup and desserts from scratch. ($)

TAIL OF THE PUP

(1152 Rte 86, Ray Brook ☎ 518.891.0777
🖰 tailofthepupbbq.com) It's hard not to be drawn into the festive atmosphere at Tail of the Pup. Located between Lake Placid and Saranac Lake in the town of Ray Brook, Tail of the Pup is a seasonal eatery with mostly outdoor seating. Their specialties include barbeque and clam bake, but the menu is extensive and offers salads, sandwiches and several items from the barbeque. Outdoor seating is under large tents and there are heaters to compensate for chilly evenings. Live local music tops off the festivities—an outdoor pool table adds to the ambiance. Tail of the Pup is a great place for families and is very kid friendly. ($/$$)

THE COTTAGE AT MIRROR LAKE INN ✪ Must See!

(77 Mirror Lake Dr. ☎ 518.523.2544 🖰 mirrorlakeinn.com) The cozy atmosphere and great view at The Cottage are hard to resist no matter what the weather is like. Located directly on Mirror Lake and part of the **Mirror Lake Inn**, the small, well-appointed pub features large picture windows and Adirondack styling. The menu is the same for lunch and dinner, and features a nice variety of salads, sandwiches and pub-style specialties. There is a large deck with a wood burning fireplace overlooking the water that doubles the seating capacity in nice weather. Menu items change periodically, and a children's menu is available. The service is friendly but expect a wait during peak seasons. A visit to the large, well-stocked bar can help pass the wait time. No reservations are accepted. ($/$$)

THE LAKE PLACID CLUB BOAT HOUSE

(654 Mirror Lake Dr. ☎ 518.523.4822 ◔ lakeplacidcp.com) The Lake Placid Club Boat House is run by the **Crowne Plaza Resort and Golf Club**. It sits right on Mirror Lake (opposite Main Street) and has terrific views of the lake and village. A seat by the window can make all the difference since the dining room is large and open. The menu is an eclectic mix. Fish, ribs, steak, pasta and even Wiener schnitzel makes an appearance. The atmosphere is lively, and it's a nice place to enjoy views of the lake at sunset. ($$)

THE VIEW RESTAURANT

(77 Mirror Lake Dr. ☎ 518.302.3000 ◔ mirrorlakeinn.com) The View Restaurant is the **Mirror Lake Inn's** casual, yet upscale dining room. The restaurant overlooks Mirror Lake and the High Peaks, and its menu includes seafood, lamb, duck, pork and vegetarian dishes. There is also an extensive wine list. The setting and service are the main attractions, and the restaurant is a good place to celebrate a special occasion. ($$$)

VERANDA

(70 Olympic Dr. ☎ 518.523.3339 ◔ lakeplacidcp.com) Slightly more upscale than most restaurants in Lake Placid, the Veranda is perched on a hill next to the **Crowne Plaza Resort** (which owns the restaurant) in a manor house that overlooks the village and Mirror Lake. The house itself is interesting and was created with special touches such as 19th century stained-glass windows imported from Germany and a cozy stone fireplace. The cuisine is traditional American and French, and the menu offers a good selection of seafood, steaks and chicken. Dinner is served Thursday through Saturday. ($$/$$$)

SURROUNDING AREA RESTAURANTS

There are many local, easy-to-reach restaurants that are outside of the Village of Lake Placid. Nearby Saranac Lake, Wilmington and Keene Valley are all an easy drive from Lake Placid and make nice options for a meal out.

AUSABLE INN DINER

(1809 NYS Rte 73, Keene Valley ☎ 518.576.9584

☷ **ausable-inn.com)** The Ausable Inn Diner is located in the Ausable Inn on the corner of Route 73 and Adirondack Street. The restaurant is warm and friendly. The lunch menu offers sandwiches and burgers, and the dinner menu features selections such as pasta, pizza, seafood, chicken and steak. There is outdoor seating in good weather. ($/$$)

CASA DEL SOL ✪ Must See!

(154 Lake Flower Ave., Saranac Lake ☎ 518.891.0977) With the arrival of a new owner in recent years, management at Casa del Sol has worked very hard to successfully overcome the unfriendly reputation of the previous proprietor. It appears they have succeeded by not only rebuilding a welcoming reputation, but in preserving some of the restaurant's traditional recipes and improving on others. The result is delicious food, and a festive, inviting atmosphere where nearly every patron

Dining

is personally greeted by the owner and served by an attentive, friendly staff.

The food is a step above your average Mexican fare with outstanding seafood combinations and a variety of sauces. Even the chips and salsa arrive with two choices of each, and the house margaritas are a refreshing ending to any activity a day in the Adirondacks can dish out. ($/$$)

EAT 'N MEET GRILL AND LARDER

(139 Broadway, Saranac Lake ☎ 518.891.3149) Eat 'n Meet is casual dining at its finest. This small yet tasteful grill is family owned and run, and visitors can watch the chef work his magic in the open kitchen while they wait. The menu offers traditional items, including gyros, fresh soups, sweet potato fries and burgers, and some not-so-common features such as calves liver, crepes, fish tacos and jerked chicken. Special requests can usually be accommodated. Seating is limited, and since the food is prepared fresh upon order, patrons should call ahead or be prepared to wait. The atmosphere is friendly, inviting and cozy at the same time. ($)

GREAT RANGE DINING

(1799 NYS Rte 73, Keene Valley ☎ 518.576.9069 ⬮ thegreatrange.com) The Great Range is a small diner in the heart of Keene Valley on Route 73. It features an eclectic dinner menu with items such as venison bangers, halibut, pasta and filet mignon. The items are tasty and the atmosphere comfortable. Over the past few years, the hours of operation have changed several times, so call ahead. Reservations for dinner are recommended. The restaurant is located next to the Adirondack Nature Conservancy. ($/$$)

HOHMEYER'S LAKE CLEAR LODGE

(6319 State Rte 30, Lake Clear ☎ 518.891.1489
☻ lodgeonlakeclear.com) The Adirondacks meet Germany at
Hohmeyer's Lake Clear Lodge. It is truly a unique and personalized dining experience. Family owned and run, Hohmeyer's
prepares Old World family recipes with Adirondack fresh
ingredients. In a cozy sitting area, guests are welcomed by the
owner in front of the fire, where they are told verbally about
the evening's selections.

Appetizers can then be ordered in the sitting area, and guests
can visit the lodge's unique, hand-built beer keller and select
a beverage from a wide assortment of imported brews. At
the guests' leisure, they can let the staff know when they are
ready to be seated for dinner in the dining room where the
personalized service continues. Hohmeyer's is a good choice
for a romantic evening or small celebration. Visitors should
bring time and be prepared for a relaxing, non-rushed evening.
($$/$$$)

LITTLE ITALY

(12 Main St., Saranac Lake ☎ 518.891.9000) Little Italy is a
local favorite for pizza and pasta. This no-frills Italian restaurant offers delicious food at a reasonable price. Located on the
corner of Main Street and Route 3, Little Italy does a thriving
carryout and dine-in business. One step inside starts the taste
buds flowing, as the smell of pizza being made right by the
front door is almost overwhelming. ($)

Dining

NONNA FINA

(151 River St., Saranac Lake ☎ 518.891.4444) Nonna Fina is a recent addition to the dining scene in Saranac Lake. In a town flooded with Italian restaurants, it took a special and experienced creator to bring something new to the table. Created by the owner of **Little Italy**, a local favorite for casual Italian fare, Nonna Fina steps the dining experience up a notch, and does so successfully with an equally tasty but slightly more refined menu.

Visitors new to the area would never guess that the building used to be a Burger King, the only remaining sign is the drive-through window on the side of the building. The rest was tastefully remodeled to provide one of the best atmospheres in town, complete with a beautiful outdoor patio overlooking Lake Flower and the public boat launch across the street. Service is professional and menu items are created with care. A personal favorite is the mushroom ravioli. ($/$$)

NOON MARK DINER

(NYS Rte 73, Keene Valley ☎ 518.576.4499
⬤ noonmarkdiner.com) The Noon Mark Diner has been a staple food establishment in Keene Valley since 1981. It serves homemade breakfast, lunch and dinner and an assortment of desserts (their milkshakes are especially delicious). The diner is located on Route 73 on the left side of the road at the far side of town, as traveled from Lake Placid. ($)

Shopping and Retail Services

Lake Placid is a great place to shop. Main Street is full of fun and interesting shops, and many sell local products that are unique to the Adirondacks. Browsing the Main Street promenade is a favorite activity in Lake Placid—the variety of goods sold there make it attractive to a wide variety of tastes.

There are a handful of outlet stores located in the village on Main Street. They are housed next door to each other with the exception of the Gap Outlet, which is across the street. Some of the outlet stores include **Team USA** *(2458 Main Street)*, **Gap Outlet** *(2457 Main Street)*, **G.H. Bass** *(2466 Main Street)*, and **Izod** *(2464 Main Street)*.

SPECIALTY STORES AND BOUTIQUES

One-of-a-kind stores are the norm in Lake Placid. Most are privately owned boutiques and shops that sell unique items and locally made merchandise.

ADIRONDACK YARNS

(2241 Saranac Ave. ☎ 518.523.9230) Adirondack Yarns is a knitting store located on Saranac Avenue. The store is run by expert knitters and offers award-winning original designs. Adirondack Yarns is well stocked and the staff is friendly and helpful.

Shopping

A PLACID LIFE

(2427 Main St. ☎ 518.523.6487 ▯ aplacidlife.com) A Placid Life carries a full line of *Life is good* products. They are the sister store to the **Jake Placid Doghouse.**

BAG TIME / LAKE PLACID CLOCK & WATCH CO.

(2565 Main St. ☎ 518.523.7372) One retail space houses Bag Time, a purse boutique and the Lake Placid Clock & Watch Co. The store is located on the rounded corner of Main Street across from the municipal lot on the Mirror Lake side of the street.

BEGLIN'S LAKE PLACID JEWELRY & GIFTS

(2533 Main St. ☎ 518.523.7829 ▯ lakeplacidjewelry.com) Beglin's Lake Placid Jewelry & Gifts is a fine jewelry and gift store located on Main Street. They specialize in custom jewelry and perform repairs right in the store. They also buy and sell estate jewelry, and replace watch batteries.

BODY & SOLE

(2439 Main St. ☎ 518.523.9398 ▯ lakeplacidbodyandsole.com) Body & Sole is a women's boutique that sells clothing, lingerie, shoes, bath products and other accessories for women of all ages. The store is large and inviting, and sits adjacent to the park on Mirror Lake. The friendly staff is always ready to assist.

CINDERELLA'S

(2531 Main St. ☎ 518.523.3666) Cinderella's is a women's apparel and children's clothing boutique. They also sell jewelry, purses, hats and accessories.

DARRAH COOPER JEWELERS

(2416 Main St. ☎ 518.523.2774) Darrah Cooper Jewelers is a fine jewelry dealer located on Main Street. They offer a selection of jewelry in the store and additional items by order. The staff is helpful and knowledgeable. They can ship items to nearly any location.

IMAGINATION STATION

(2515 Main St. ☎ 518.523.4112) The Imagination Station is a fun, learning store that sells games, toys, books and local apparel. Visitors are invited to try out some toys in the store, such as rubber band guns.

JAKE PLACID DOGHOUSE

(2439 Main St. ☎ 518.523.6701 🖰 jakeplaciddoghouse.com) Jake Placid Doghouse's slogan is "Stuff that Makes Dogs Happy." This fun canine-oriented store is run by the owners of **A Placid Life** (aka *Life is good.*), located a few storefronts up the street. The dog store is their original location and Jake is their wirehaired fox terrier who can often be found in the store. The Jake Placid Doghouse sells a great selection of dog treats, toys and accessories, and is a local favorite for dog lovers.

JUST BEAD IT

(2573 Main St., Ste 1 ☎ 518.523.0064) Just Bead It is a bead store located on the rounded corner of Main Street across from the municipal parking lot. Visitors can enjoy looking through hundreds of beads from around the world and speaking with the designer/owner for ideas. Worktables are also available for in-store creation.

LAKE PLACID ANTIQUE CENTER

(2513 Main St. ☎ 518.523.3913) The Lake Placid Antique Center is located on Main Street. They offer stained glass, lamps and furnishings. Their sister store, A Touch of Glass, is located on Parkside Drive and offers a variety of stained-glass work.

LAKE PLACID CHRISTMAS COMPANY

(2435 Main St. ☎ 518.523.8210) The Lake Placid Christmas Company sells a large assortment of holiday items including ornaments, Department 56 Villages, candles and other festive items. They ship merchandise to any location.

LOCAL COLOR

(2505 Main St. ☎ 518.523.3006) Local Color is a small upscale ladies boutique located on the Mirror Lake side of Main Street. They sell mainly clothes, hats and jewelry.

LOG CABIN ANTIQUES

(2488 Main St. ☎ 518.523.3225) Log Cabin Antiques offers a selection of antiques and handmade household items. They are located on Main Street.

NEWMAN'S NEWS

(2523 Main St., Ste 2 ☎ 518.523.3536) Newman's News is a well-stocked news and magazine store located in the middle of Main Street on the Mirror Lake side of the road. They sell newspapers, magazines, snacks, beverages, and travel essentials such as aspirin and shampoo. The owner is friendly and helpful to visitors.

OLYMPIC REGIONAL DEVELOPMENT AUTHORITY STORE

(2426 Main St. ☎ 518.523.1420 🖳 whiteface.com) The ORDA store, centrally located on Main Street in Lake Placid, provides information on events taking place at the Olympic venues. Visitors can purchase lift tickets, pick up event schedules and purchase the popular Olympic Site Passport. The passport provides access to all Olympic venues at a discounted price. Passports are also available at venue ticket offices.

RUTHIE'S RUN

(2415 Main St. ☎ 518.523.3271) Ruthie's Run is a sportswear and skiwear boutique located on Main Street. The store originally opened in 1968 as Thaire's Ski Shop. The current owners have had the shop since 1984. They sell both men's and women's clothing, skiwear and accessories. Some of the specialties include M. Miller jackets, coats, vests and ski parkas.

SUMMER ANTIQUES

(2517 Main St. ☎ 518.523.1876 🖳 summerantiques.com) Summer Antiques is an antique store located on Main Street. They focus primarily on items such as period furniture, early paintings, mission oak furniture, sports memorabilia and other collectibles. Many items are from Northern New York and New England.

U.S. OLYMPIC SPIRIT STORE

(U.S. Olympic Training Ctr. ☎ 518.523.2600) The U.S Olympic Spirit Store offers a great selection of official U.S. Olympic memorabilia and clothing. They are located in the lobby of the **U.S. Olympic Training Center**. This is the only store in Lake

Shopping

Placid where each purchase directly supports the U.S. Olympic athletes.

THE BOOKSTORE PLUS

(2491 Main St. ☎ 518.523.2950 ☗ thebookstoreplus.com) The Bookstore Plus is a family-owned-and-operated independent bookstore located on Main Street in the heart of the village. The owners do a nice job stocking the shelves with local titles and books that tie in with local events. The store also sells a variety of stationery, music and art supplies.

THE FALLEN ARCH

(2537 Main St. ☎ 518.523.5310 ☗ thefallenarch.com) The Fallen Arch on Main Street sells athletic shoes and apparel. They specialize in running shoes but also sell boots, socks, clothes and accessories. The Fallen Arch is located a few storefronts up from the Golden Arrow Lakeside Resort on the Mirror Lake side of the road.

THE GLASSBLOWING SHOP

(Alpine Mall, 2525 Main St., Ste 2 ☎ 518.523.8750 ☗ theglassblowingshop.com) The Glassblowing Shop offers hand-blown gifts and art designs. The shop is located in the Alpine Mall but also has an entrance on Main Street. Daily demonstrations are given.

THE LAKE PLACID MARKET

(2501 Main St. ☎ 518.523.3558) The Lake Placid Market is a gallery and boutique that sells art, decorative gifts and other items such as Vera Bradley purses.

Kayaking in the Adirondacks (© Michaela Gaaserud)

Downtown Saranac Lake (© Michaela Gaaserud)

Whiteface Mountain (© *Shutterstock/Yulia Ivanova*)

Adirondack Balloon Festival (© Shutterstock/Jim Lozouski)

Mirror Lake (© Shutterstock/Juan Vte. Muñoz)

Ausable River *(© Michaela Gaaserud)*

Whiteface Mountain and Lake Placid *(© Shutterstock/Jason Jr)*

el. 4867ft. 1483.5m. WHITEFACE MT.

Lake Placid Main Street *(© Michaela Gaaserud)*

Olympic Ski Jump (© *Shutterstock/ Steve Broer*)

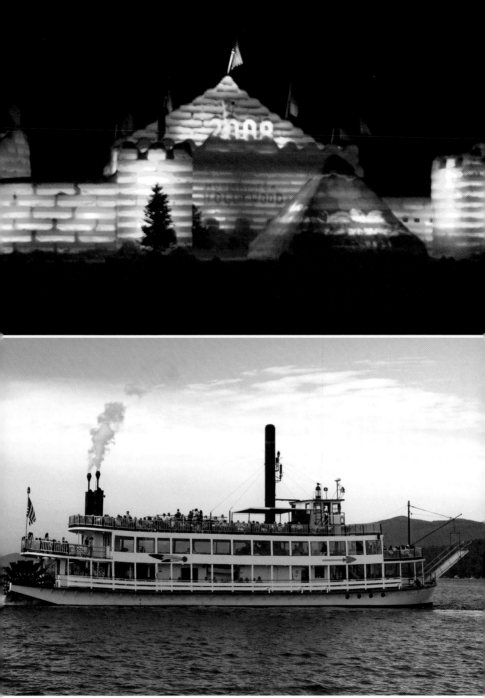

Ice Castle During Saranac Lake Winter Carnival *(© Michaela Gaaserud)*

Lake George Sightseeing Boat *(© Shutterstock/Vlad Ghiea)*

Weather Station at Whiteface Summit (© Michaela Gaaserud)

TIBET ASIAN HIMALAYAN GIFTS & HANDICRAFTS

(Alpine Mall) The Tibet Asian Himalayan Gifts & Handicrafts is, as the name suggests, is a small craft store selling items of Tibet, Asian and Himalayan nature including clothing. They are located in the Alpine Mall on the Mirror Lake side of Main Street

VILLAGE COMFORTS

(Alpine Mall, 2527 Main St. ☎ 518.523.2402) Village Comforts is a fabric, fine linen and quilt shop located in the Alpine Mall. They also sell unique gifts and home accessories.

WHERE'D YOU GET THAT HAT?

(2569 Main St. ☎ 518.523.3101 ⬤ wheredyougetthathat.com)
Where'd you get that Hat? is a hat boutique on Main Street with a 20-plus-year history. They offer an amazing selection of headwear for all occasions and tastes. They stock cowboy hats, stocking hats, ski hats, caps and so on. They also have a children's boutique inside the store called Jaxx and an online store.

SPECIALTY FOOD STORES

Visitors craving a special treat don't have far to search in Lake Placid. There are candy stores, dessert stores, wine stores and even a popcorn store. There are also a handful of organic and health food shops in the village, which are gaining popularity with both residents and tourists.

CANDY MAN

(2465 Main St. ☎ 800.232.4626 ⬤ candymanonline.com)
Candy Man is a Lake Placid staple in the village since 1977.

They hand make a large assortment of delicious Adirondack Chocolates daily using fresh ingredients and original recipes. Other candy is also available in the store. World-class athletes have been spotted coming out of Candy Man with bags filled with chocolate—it is that good. They also have an online store and another, larger retail store on Route 86 in the heart of Wilmington.

GOOSE WATCH WINERY TASTING ROOM

(Alpine Mall, 2523 Main St. ☎ 518.523.1955 ☔ goosewatch.com) Goose Watch Winery, located in the Finger Lakes region of New York, offers a tasting room in the Village of Lake Placid. Goose Watch produces wine from classic European varieties of grapes including Viognier, Pinot Grigio, Lemberger, and Merlot. Gifts and wine baskets are also sold at the tasting room.

GREEN GODDESS NATURAL FOODS

(183 Newman Rd. ☎ 518.523.4676 ☔ greengoddessfoods.com) Green Goddess is an organic and natural foods store. They specialize in the sale of locally grown or produced products from the North Country and New England. They also sell supplements.

SOUTH MEADOWS FARM MAPLE SUGARWORKS

(67 Sugarworks Way ☎ 518.523.9369 ☔ maplesyrup.net) South Meadows Farm runs a small maple sugarworks store at their farm on Route 73. Located four miles outside of the Village of Lake Placid, the atmospheric little store offers high-quality maple syrup and other maple products. They also offer jams, pancake mix, candy and other delectable items.

SUGAR SHACK DESSERT CO.

(2567 Main St. ☎ 518.523.7540) The Sugar Shack Dessert Co. is a sweet little dessert shop located near the rounded corner of Main Street on the Mirror Lake side of the road. Visitors can take a break from an active day in the Adirondacks with a snack or fresh cup of hot chocolate made from scratch.

SWEDISH HILL WINERY TASTING ROOM

(121 Cascade Rd. ☎ 518.523.2498 🖰 swedishhill.com) Swedish Hill Winery, located in the Finger Lakes region of New York, offers more than 20 wines for tasting and sale at their Lake Placid location on Route 73. The helpful staff is available to assist visitors in selecting specific wines to taste, and they enjoy sharing their knowledge. Gifts are also available at the tasting room.

TEMPTATIONS FROM LAKE PLACID GOURMET

(2509 Main St. ☎ 518.523.3434) Temptations from Lake Placid Gourmet is a tempting little sweet shop on Main Street that sells items such as small cakes, cheese and jelly. The friendly owner is happy to answer any questions and assist with selections.

THE ADIRONDACK POPCORN CO.

(2520 Main St. ☎ 518.837.5277 🖰 adirondackpopcorn.com) The Adirondack Popcorn Co. offers a fun selection of fresh popcorn made right in the store. Moose crunch is a local favorite flavor and includes chocolate, caramel corn and pretzels.

GIFTS AND SOUVENIRS

Gift and souvenir stores take all forms in Lake Placid. In general, they are a step above traditional tourist town merchants and their proprietors go the extra mile to make their stores warm and inviting in the Adirondack tradition.

ADIRONDACK MUSEUM ON MAIN STORE AND GALLERY

(2477 Main St. ☎ 518.523.9074) The Adirondack Museum on Main Store and Gallery is run by the Adirondack Museum. It offers items such as rustic crafts, jewelry, art and books.

CRITTERS

(2527 Main St. ☎ 518.523.1177) Critters is a gift shop that sells local apparel such as T-shirts and sweatshirts. They also carry a selection of Lake Placid and Adirondack souvenirs. Critters has a storefront on Main Street and a side entrance in the Alpine Mall (the Alpine Mall entrance is located on Main Street on the Mirror Lake side of the road).

FANFARE OF LAKE PLACID, LLC

(2423 Main St. ☎ 518.523.9223 ✆ fanfarelp.com) Fanfare has offered unique gifts and souvenirs in Lake Placid for more than 25 years. They are a family-owned business located on Main Street. Some of the items they carry include: T-shirts, moccasins, home accessories, toys, maple products and the ever-popular "moose poop."

FORTUNES OF TIME

(2519 Main St. ☎ 518.523.4886) Fortunes of Time is a cozy gift shop on Main Street that offers items such as local apparel,

Shopping

candles, vintage-style signs and jewelry. The shop is warm and inviting, and often smells like maple syrup.

HIGH PEAKS GIFT SHOP

(2527 Main St., Suite 1 ☎ 518.523.2371) The High Peaks Gift Shop sells local apparel and other gifts. They have an entrance on Main Street and also in the Alpine Mall.

TWO HARTS

(2523 Main St. ☎ 518.523.3840) Two Harts sells jewelry, women's clothes, purses, and music group items such as Grateful Dead T-shirts. They are located on Main Street on the Mirror Lake side of the road.

ARTS AND CRAFT GALLERIES

There is no shortage of fine galleries and craft stores in Lake Placid. They range from casual locally made merchandise to high-end art stores.

511 GALLERY

(2461 Main St. ☎ 518.523.7163 ☷ 511gallery.com) The 511 Gallery is a formal art gallery affiliated with the 511 Gallery in New York City. They feature contemporary art and focus on works from emerging artists from the United States and overseas. Their artwork is high end and includes painting, sculpture, photography and installation art.

A POINT OF VIEW GALLERY

(6047 Sentinel Rd. ☎ 518.837.5124) A Point of View Gallery opened in early 2008 and is located on Sentinel Road in the renovated bottom floor of a house. The gallery shows work from local artists and is run by a well-known Adirondack photographer. Handcrafted framing is also available at the gallery, along with large-format printing.

BRUSH ON IN

(2520 Main St. ☎ 518.523.6554) Brush On In is a ceramic studio where visitors can paint their own pottery. They specialize in group activities or painting for individuals. They have more than 200 pieces of ceramic to choose from. They glaze and fire each piece, and prepare them for pickup or shipping.

GUY BREWSTER HUGHES ART GALLERY

(Lake Placid Public Library, 2471 Main Street ☎ 518.523.3200 ⬛ lakeplacidlibrary.org) The Guy Brewster Hughes Art Gallery is located inside the public library in Lake Placid on Main Street. Hughes was a watercolorist in the Adirondacks whose wish was to have a space in the public library to display local artists. The gallery is a fulfillment of that wish, and the work of many talented artists are featured in the gallery.

MOON TREE DESIGNS

(422 Main St. ☎ 518.523.1970) Moon Tree Design is a high-end craft gallery/gift shop located on Main Street. They offer unique pottery, jewelry and handmade household items.

THE V GALLERY

(2413 Main St.) The V Gallery features local artists from Northern New York and the Adirondacks. It is located on Main Street across from the **High Peaks Resort**.

ADIRONDACK FURNISHINGS

Adirondack furnishings are sold in many stores in and around Lake Placid. Most are made from local materials, but some larger stores distribute goods from other regions. As a rule of thumb, the stores right in the village will have higher prices than those in the outlying areas. They will often have a greater variety of merchandise as well, so it can be a trade-off. What visitors will find if they take the time to shop around the region is that locally made furnishings are often sold right from their creators' homes and garages, and from small retail stores. Many hidden gems and very reasonable prices can be found for those willing to invest the time to look.

ADIRONDACK DECORATIVE ARTS & CRAFTS

(2512 Main St. ☎ 518.523.4545) Adirondack Decorative Arts & Crafts is a well-stocked, three-story rustic furnishing store located in the middle of the village on Main Street. They carry a large assortment of local style furnishings, gifts and housewares. They also have a smaller gift shop just across the street called the Adirondack Trading Company. This store carries Adirondack souvenirs, local foods and clothing. Both stores are very popular, and the staff is friendly and knowledgeable.

ADIRONDACK STORE

(2024 Saranac Ave. ☎ 518.523.2646
🖱 theadirondackstore.com) The Adirondack Store offers rustic furniture, china, birch furnishing, camp blankets and many accessories. They are located on Saranac Avenue and also offer interior design services.

Shopping

GEORGE JAQUES RUSTIC FURNITURE

(Rte 73, Keene Valley ☎ 518.576.2214 📱 georgejaques.com)
George Jaques Rustic Furniture in Keene Valley has a history
dating back to 1920. It is a family-run business and the product
of three generations of furniture builders. They specialize in
quality Great Camp–style furniture with a particular emphasis
on dining furniture, but also make furniture for all home
and camp rooms. Furniture made by George Jaques Rustic
Furniture can be found in high-end Adirondack resorts such as
The Point and the **Lake Placid Lodge**.

MOODY TREE FARM

(60 County Rte 55, Saranac Lake ☎ 518.891.2468
📱 **moodytreefarm.com)** The Moody Tree farm offers a traditional holiday experience of cutting your own Christmas
tree. They also offer beautiful, well-priced balsam products
including wreaths, garlands, and so on, made right at their
farm. Other holiday decorations are also available, and items
can be made to order. They also offer a variety of other home
accessories and gifts. The farm is located between Saranac Lake
and Gabriels.

RESTORED STORAGE CHESTS

(Rte 86, Gabriels) There is no official sign or advertisement for
a little-known shop in the tiny town of Gabriels, not far from
Saranac Lake. There's just an old theatre with a masonry stair-
case leading up to a large door. If the door is open, the store is
open—and sometimes there's even an "open" sign. Inside, visitors will find a large room full of beautifully restored antique
chests. Some are roll-top, others not. Each piece is carefully
restored by a friendly gentleman who will most likely be there

Shopping

with his dog. The prices are very reasonable compared to what
you would find in an antique store and the workmanship is
first rate. From Saranac Lake, take Route 86 north to Gabriels.
Upon entering Gabriels (don't blink), the store is located
around the bend on the left side of the road prior to the intersection of Rainbow Lake Road.

RICE FURNITURE

**(34 Main St., Saranac Lake ☎ 518.891.4170
☋ ricefurniture.info)** Rice Furniture is a complete home
furnishing center located in Saranac Lake. They offer traditional Adirondack-style furniture and also bedding, flooring
and accessories.

THE RAY BROOK FROG

(Rte 86, Ray Brook ☎ 518.891.3333 ☋ raybrookfrog.com) The
Ray Brook Frog, located in Ray Brook (between Lake Placid
and Saranac Lake), offers a wide selection of rustic-style
hickory furniture, and indoor and outdoor lighting. They also
showcase furniture crafted by local Adirondack artists.

TWIGS RUSTIC GALLERY

(5730 Cascade Rd. ☎ 518.523.5361) Twigs Rustic Gallery is
located a little off the main drag on Cascade Road. They have
a nice selection of antiques, rustic furnishings, vintage collect-
ables and household items for an Adirondack decor. The staff
is friendly, and there is a large selection of items to choose
from.

FARMERS MARKETS

Farmers markets are extremely popular in the Adirondacks, especially given the short growing season. Locally grown produce can be found alongside baked goods and sometimes even local furnishings and crafts. If visitors look hard enough, a local farmers market can be found on almost any day of the week during the summer and some extend into the colder months by moving indoors.

KEENE FARMERS MARKET

(Rte 73, Marcy Airfield, Keene ☎ 518.561.7167) The Keene Farmers Market is held mid-June through the beginning of October on Sunday mornings at the Marcy Airfield. They offer fresh produce, crafts and gifts.

LAKE PLACID FARMERS MARKET

(Lake Placid Center for the Arts, 17 Algonquin Dr.
☎ 518.523.2512 ◕ lakeplacidfarmersmarket.com) The Lake Placid Farmers Market is held every Wednesday from late June through Mid-October at the **Lake Placid Center for the Arts**. The event is held rain or shine, and offers vegetables, fruit, artisanal organic cheese, free-range chicken and eggs, grass-fed beef and pork, fresh baked goods, snacks and crafts. An indoor Harvest Market is also held from late October through mid-December on Saturdays at the Center.

PAUL SMITH'S FARMERS MARKET

(Paul Smith's College, Rte 86 and Rte 30, Paul Smiths
☎ 518.891.7194) Paul Smith's Farmers Market is held mid-June through September on Friday afternoons at the college.

It features vegetables, berries, baked goods, herbs, jams and grass-fed lamb.

SARANAC LAKE VILLAGE FARMERS MARKET

(Riverside Park, Corner of Rte 3 and Main St. Saranac Lake ☎ 518.834.7306 📍 saranaclakevillagefarmersmarket.com) The Saranac Lake Village Farmers Market is held in downtown Saranac Lake on Saturdays from June through mid-October. The market is organized by the Ausable Valley Grange and offers organic vegetables, baked goods, dairy products, meat, wine, pottery and handcrafted goods. An indoor Harvest Market is also offered from mid-October through May.

SPAS AND SALONS

There are multiple spas and salons on and near Main Street. Visitors are advised to call ahead for appointments.

BALANCED BODYWORK & MASSAGE OF LAKE PLACID

(2733 Main St. ☎ 518.523.3780 📍 placidbodywork.com) Balanced Bodywork & Massage of Lake Placid offers professional massage therapy for relaxation, recovery and pain relief. They take appointments seven days a week and will even travel to private homes.

CRISPIN HAIR DESIGN & SPA

(Alpine Mall, 2527 Main St., Ste 4 ☎ 518.523.9736) Crispin Hair Design & Spa offers hair cutting and styling, and spa services such as facials, nails and waxing. They also offer massage therapy.

LAKE PLACID SPEEDY SPA

(1975 Saranac Ave. ☎ 518.523.5500 🦷 lpspeedyspa.com) Lake Placid Speedy Spa is a day spa offering massage, waxing and facials. They employ friendly staff and experienced massage therapists.

MARTINA'S EUROPEAN SKIN CARE

(2511 Main St. ☎ 518.523.7546) Martina's European Skin Care is a beauty salon and skin-care specialist. They are conveniently located on Main Street.

MIRROR LAKE INN RESORT AND SPA ✪ Must See!

(Mirror Lake Dr. ☎ 518.523.2544) The Spa at the Mirror Lake Inn offers a full line of professional spa services. Their staff is well trained, friendly and professional. They are a top-notch spa conveniently located in the village. They have many repeat customers and patrons do not need to be inn guests.

RIVER ROCK SALON INC.

(263 Station St., Ste 3 ☎ 518.523.4400 🦷 riverrocksalon.com) The River Rock Salon is a certified Eminence Green Salon. They offer hair design, facials, hair removal, alternative treatments and wedding preparation.

OUTDOOR GEAR AND GUIDING

As could be expected, there are numerous outdoor equipment retailers and guiding services in Lake Placid and the surrounding area. The sizes of the stores vary. There are chain retailers such as Eastern Mountain Sports (EMS) right on Main Street, but more often than not, small, well-stocked privately owned and run shops are the norm.

Equipment rental businesses are easy to find in Lake Placid. Many visitors opt not to bring heavy equipment for sports activities—such as skis, kayaks and bicycles—when traveling and rely on local shops for leasing gear.

As for guiding services, the vast wilderness is often best explored with a professional. Finding a lost hiker or injured climber in six million acres can be like finding a needle in a haystack. There are many knowledgeable and friendly professionals available to help get the most out of an outdoor adventure. A large percentage of guides in the Lake Placid area grew up in the Adirondacks, and the knowledge and experience they can pass on can easily outweigh the cost of their services.

Please see the chapters on "Summer Activities" and "Winter Activities" for businesses that cater to specific sports.

EASTERN MOUNTAIN SPORTS (EMS)

(2453 Main St. ☎ 518.523.2505 🖱 ems.com) Eastern Mountain Sports (EMS) is an East Coast chain selling outdoor equipment and clothing. They offer a local rock climbing and adventure school that includes guided climbs, guided hikes, family programs, mountain biking and rappelling. They are accredited by the American Mountain Guides Association.

JONES OUTFITTERS, LTD.

(2733 Main St. ☎ 518.523.3468 🖱 jonesoutfitters.com) Jones Outfitters sells fly-fishing gear, paddling gear, dog supplies and outdoor clothing. They are located on Main Street. Jones

Outfitters also offers fly-fishing instruction, guided fishing trips, and canoe and kayak rentals.

BEAR CUB ADVENTURE TOURS

(☎ 518.523.4339 ☗ mountain-air.com/canoeing) Bear Cub Adventure Tours provides year-round outdoor guiding and instruction on a variety of outdoor skills. Some of their offerings include wilderness canoe trips, paddling instruction, fishing trips, backcountry skiing and telemark, snowshoe tours, and ice fishing.

HIGH PEAKS MOUNTAIN GUIDES

(2733 Main St. ☎ 518.523.3764 ☗ hpmountainguides.com) High Peaks Mountain Adventures is a resource center for trip planning and guiding in the Adirondacks. They offer outdoor activities for individuals and groups, such as rock climbing, biking, canoeing, hiking, ice climbing, backcountry skiing and kayaking. Trips are led by certified instructors who are knowledgeable about the area. High Peaks Mountain Guides is located at the **High Peaks Cyclery** on Main Street. They also offer group-style lodging.

Summer Activities

There is simply nothing equal to summers in Lake Placid. Even a well-seasoned couch potato will find it difficult to stay indoors with all the activities that lie beyond the front steps. The following is information on some of the most popular summer recreation activities available in and around Lake Placid. Businesses that offer equipment and services for these activities are also included in this chapter.

Many specialty stores that are difficult to find in other parts of the country are located in the Adirondacks, such as mountaineering equipment stores and retailers specializing in fly fishing.

BOATING

Boating is one of the top pastimes in the Adirondacks in the warmer months. There is an endless supply of navigable waterways in and around Lake Placid. Visitors bringing their own boats can take advantage of many public boat launches in the park. Some offer hard-surface ramps for trailers while others are designed as hand launches for nonmotorized boats.

Several local marinas and outfitters offer short-term boat rentals. Prices range widely depending on the type of watercraft but most offer convenient locations and easy access.

CASCADE LAKES BOAT LAUNCH

(Rte 73, Keene) There is a hand launch site for the majestic Cascade Lakes off Route 73 (six miles northwest of Keene), with parking for 15 cars. No motorized boats are allowed.

LAKE COLBY BOAT LAUNCH

(Rte 86, Saranac Lake) A hand launch is located two miles north of the Village of Saranac Lake on Lake Colby (across from the hospital), with parking for 30 cars and trailers. There is a 10 hp motor restriction on the lake.

LAKE FLOWER BOAT LAUNCH

(Rte 86, Saranac Lake) The Lake Flower Boat Launch is located right in the Village of Saranac Lake in the public park. It offers a hard-surface launch for motorboats, and parking for 21 cars and trailers. The ramp provides access to miles of waterways including the Saranac Lakes. Some routes require boating through locks.

LAKE PLACID BOAT LAUNCH

(Mirror Lake Dr.) There is a nice public boat launch on Lake Placid off Route 86 on Mirror Lake Drive. It is a hard surface launch for trailers carrying motorized boats and there is parking for 25 cars and trailers.

MIRROR LAKE BOAT LAUNCH

(Mirror Lake Dr.) Mirror Lake offers a hand launch site for nonmotorized boats and electric motors. There is parking for 25 cars and a 50-yard carry is required to the water. The launch is located off Route 86 in the village.

CAPTAIN MARNEY'S BOAT RENTALS

(3 Victor Herbert Rd. ☎ 518.523.9746) Captain Marney's Boat Rentals offers motorboats, fishing boats, pontoon boats, kayaks and canoes for rent on Lake Placid. They also rent water skis. ($/$$)

MIRROR LAKE BOAT RENTALS

(One Main St. ☎ 518.524.7890) Mirror Lake Boat Rentals offers electric boats, sailboats, kayaks, canoes, rowboats and paddleboats for rent on Mirror Lake. They have a dock right on the water and are easy to find. They also rent electric cruiser cars (for land use). Beware, they charge a $2 cranky fee for whining and complaining. ($/$$)

BIRD WATCHING

The many bogs and upland boreal habitats located in the Lake Placid area make it an ideal location for birding. Some species summer in the Adirondacks while others make it their winter home. The population is always changing, which makes birding year-round an exciting pastime. Some unique species found in the Adirondacks include the loon, spruce grouse, peregrine falcon, three-toed woodpecker, and ruby-crowned kinglet.

ADIRONDACK HIGH PEAKS WILDERNESS AREA

(South of Rte 73, between Lake Placid and Keene Valley) The Adirondack High Peaks Wilderness Area is the largest designated wilderness area in New York. It is considered an important birding area with its mixed forest.

WILMINGTON NOTCH

(Off Rte 86, just south of Wilmington) The cliffs and bluffs in this area are good for spotting birds of prey. Examples of the inhabitants of this area include peregrine falcon, hawks and ravens.

BLOOMINGDALE BOG

North of Saranac Lake off Route 86 and west of Bloomingdale on Route 81 is a four-mile trail through the Bloomingdale Bog. This area is a lowland boreal wetland where bird watchers can find boreal chickadees, black-backed woodpeckers, flycatchers, palm warblers, and Lincoln's sparrow.

CLIMBING AND MOUNTAINEERING

The High Peaks is a prime destination in the East for rock climbing, ice climbing, and mountaineering. Hundreds of climbing routes traverse the mountainsides. Popular climbs such as those near the Cascade Lakes are easily accessible from the roadside and others, such as the famous Wallface Mountain (the biggest wilderness cliff in the East at over 700 feet high) are located in the remote backcountry. Slide climbs are also plentiful and provide stunning views.

Many of the region's guiding services are located in either Keene Valley or Keene. Both are a short drive from Lake Placid. There are also guidebooks available in Lake Placid for climbing routes in the region.

ADIRONDACK ROCK AND RIVER GUIDE SERVICE, INC.

(Keene ☎ 518.576.2041 ⬤ rockandriver.com) Adirondack Rock and River Guide Service, Inc., provides licensed professionals to guide rock climbing, ice climbing, summer mountaineering and winter mountaineering in the High Peaks. Their facilities include an indoor climbing wall and lodging for the general public. They have been in business since 1988 and are accredited by the American Mountain Guides Association (AMGA).

Adirondack Rock and River also provides group guiding and instruction. ($$/$$$)

ALPINE ADVENTURES, INC.
(10873 Rte 9N, Keene ☎ 518.576.9881

🖰 alpineadven.com) Alpine Adventures offers guided rock and ice climbing, backcountry skiing and mountaineering. They also offer private instruction and scheduled courses. Alpine Adventures is located in Keene and was founded in 1985. The business is family owned and operated. ($$/$$$)

CLOUDSPLITTER MOUNTAIN GUIDES LLC
(Rte 73, Keene Valley ☎ 518.569.8910

🖰 cloudsplitterguides.com) Cloudsplitter Mountain Guides supplies AMGA-certified rock climbing instruction, ice climbing instruction, guiding, backcountry ski tours, summit climbs and select alpine climbing. They also offer skills workshops and group climbing tours. ($$/$$$)

THE MOUNTAINEER
(1866 NYS Rte 73 Keene Valley ☎ 518.576.2281

🖰 mountaineer.com) The Mountaineer is one of the best outdoor stores in the region for climbing and mountaineering gear. They are located in the heart of the High Peaks in Keene Valley and are a wonderful resource for information on rock climbing, ice climbing and hiking in the area. They also sell top-notch outdoor gear, books and apparel, and the staff is extremely knowledgeable and helpful.

CYCLING (ROAD)

The Lake Placid has become a training ground for avid cyclers. Road bikers, triathletes, and recreational cyclers come to the area to take advantage of wide road shoulders, incredible scenery and challenging hills. Many of the road surfaces are smooth, and the back roads see little traffic.

Riders should pick up a good map of the area before heading out, but with that in hand, the opportunities are endless. Ride past rivers, mountains, Olympic venues, forest and meadows—visitors can ride for days without repeating routes. One of the most popular routes is the 56-mile **Ironman USA** course that starts and ends in the village.

HIGH PEAKS CYCLERY
(2733 Main St. ☎ 518.523.3764 ● highpeakscyclery.com)
The High Peaks Cyclery is located on Main Street. They sell mountain bicycles, road bicycles, triathlon bikes, Nordic skis and accessories. They also rent bikes, as well as climbing and Nordic equipment. The High Peaks Cyclery runs the mountain bike park at the **Olympic Sports Complex** in the summer and also sponsors many local biking events.

PLACID PLANET BICYCLES
(2242 Saranac Ave. ☎ 518.523.4128

● placidplanetbicycles.com) Placid Planet Bicycles is a full-service bike shop just off Main Street on Saranac Avenue. They offer sales, rentals, and bicycle maintenance and repair. They also sell bike apparel and accessories. The friendly staff is very knowledgeable and bends over backward to accommodate their customers even when the store is busy in the peak season.

FISHING

The Adirondacks is the premier fishing destination in the eastern United States. Thousands of waterways including lakes, ponds, rivers and streams lure countless anglers to the Adirondacks each year. The Ausable River is famous for its brown trout and is considered to be one of the prime trout streams in the United States. Other catches include bass, walleye, splake, rainbow trout, salmon and panfish.

The Adirondack Regional Tourism Council publishes a brochure titled, *Adirondack Fishing—An Angler's Guide to the Adirondack Lakes, Ponds, Rivers and Streams.* This is a very helpful guide that includes grid listings for guide services, charters, bait and tackle shops, boat launches and marinas in the Adirondacks. It can be obtained through the council's website *(visitadirondacks. com)*.

Valid fishing licenses are required in New York. They can be obtained from the town clerk on Main Street in Lake Placid.

ADIRONDACK FISHING INC.
**(549 State Rte 86, Paul Smiths ☎ 518.327.3133
 adirondackfishing.net)** Adirondack Fishing Inc. provides guided fishing trips in Lake Placid, Saranac Lake and Paul Smith's. They fish both cold and warm-water species. Trips are run from a 16-foot Lund boat. ($$)

FLY FISH THE ADIRONDACKS GUIDE SERVICE
(Richard Garfield ☎ 518.637.2124 flyfishtheadirondacks.com)
Fly Fish the Adirondacks Guide Service offers personalized fly-fishing trips and instruction near Lake Placid on the West

Branch of the Ausable River, and on the Saranac River, Salmon River, Raquette River, Chateaugay River and St. Regis River. The company is a one-man show with the owner providing all personalized services. Current rates and booking information can be found on their website. ($$)

HIGH PEAKS GUIDE SERVICE

(High Peaks Region ☎ 518.396.9503 highpeaksguideservice.com) High Peaks Guide Service offers guided fishing trips in the High Peaks region. They specialize in custom outings. Their guide is state licensed and has more than 20 years experience. They also offer guided hunting trips. ($$)

HUNGRY TROUT FLY SHOP

(5239 Rte 86, Wilmington ☎ 518.946.2117 hungrytrout.com) The Hungry Trout Fly Shop is a one-stop fly-fishing resource located in Wilmington by the Ausable River. They offer a large selection of flies, guiding, instruction, and gear for sale and rent.

PLACID BAY VENTURES OUTDOOR GUIDE SERVICE

(2187 Saranac Ave. ☎ 518.523.2001 placidbay.com) Placid Bay Ventures Outdoor Guide Service offers guided fly-fishing instruction and outings. All instruction is private. They also offer fly-fishing packages and discounts on lodging at **Placid Bay Inn** on Lake Placid. ($$)

WILEY'S FLIES

(379 County Rd. 60, Rainbow Lake ☎ 518.891.1829 wileysflies.com) Wiley's Flies offers guided fly-fishing trips on the Ausable River and on a number of other rivers near the Lake Placid area. They offer custom trips by a renowned fly tyer and author. Their shop is located in Rainbow Lake, 20 miles northwest of Lake Placid. ($$)

GOLF

The Adirondacks are known as a prime golf destination. Several world-class golf courses dot the landscape as testament to a long history of the sport in the region. Well-known golfers such as Craig Wood, Seymour Dunn and Alistair MacKenzie assisted with the development of golf in Lake Placid and the design of some of the finest courses available to the public today.

LAKE PLACID CLUB MOUNTAIN COURSE ✪ Must See!
(88 Morningside Dr. ☎ 518.523.4460

🖰 lakeplacidcp.com/golf.html) The Lake Placid Mountain Course is a fully irrigated 18-hole, par 70, 6,156-yard golf course. It was originally designed in 1910 but was renovated in 1931 by Alistair MacKenzie, creator of the Augusta National course. The course was designed to take advantage of the surrounding scenery, and features small greens and tree-lined fairways. The course has more to offer strong players with a straight shot, but the breathtaking views and interesting design will appeal to all players. The course is open May through November. ($/$$)

LAKE PLACID LINKS COURSE
(Crowne Plaza – Lake Placid Club, 88 Morningside Dr.
☎ 518.523.4460 🖰 lakeplacidcp.com/golf.html) The Links Course, an 18-hole, par 71, 7,006-yard golf course boasts a Scottish-style design that is longer and less hilly than the

Mountain Course. It has undulating greens, native fescue grass and fairways full of bunkers. Rated as four stars by *Golf Digest*, the course is known to have wonderful scenery and a challenging design. ($$)

LAKE PLACID CLUB RESORT, EXECUTIVE COURSE

(Crowne Plaza – Lake Placid Club, 88 Morningside Dr.
☎ **518.523.4460** ☋ **lakeplacidcp.com/golf.html)** The Executive Course, also known as the Pristine Nine, is a nine-hole course and the third in the Lake Placid Club's trio. It is an excellent course for beginners and has seven par 3s and two par 4s. ($)

CRAIG WOOD GOLF COURSE

(Cascade Rd. ☎ **518.523.9811** ☋ **craigwoodgolfclub.com)** The Craig Wood golf course was originally completed as a nine-hole course in 1925, but was soon expanded to an 18-hole course. It is a par 72, 6,554-yard course, and is currently run by the Town of North Elba. The course has a number of memorable holes and is considered to be challenging. Named after Master/U.S. Open Champion Craig Wood, it was designed by Seymour Dunn. ($/$$)

SARANAC INN GOLF COURSE

(125 County Rte 46, Saranac Lake ☎ **518.891.1402**
☋ **saranacinn.com)** Saranac Inn is an 18-hole, par 72, 6,631-yard golf course. Located on the shores of Upper Saranac Lake, it is meticulously maintained and provides a variety of scenery throughout the course. The course was designed by Seymour Dunn, a well-known Scottish designer, and is known for its state-of-the-art equipment and excellent reputation. ($$)

WHITEFACE CLUB AND RESORT GOLF COURSE

(373 Whiteface Inn Ln. ☎ 518.523.2551

🌐 whitefaceclubresort.com) The Whiteface Club and Resort Golf Course was established in 1898 and is an 18-hole, par 71, 6,451-yard course. It is located on the shores of Lake Placid and was designed by architect John Van Kleek with the assistance of a well-known consultant Walter Hagen. The result is said to be the "quintessential Adirondack course," mostly due to the outstanding lake and mountain views from the course, and the fact that it is challenging to even the best players. ($$/$$$)

HIKING

There are far too many hikes in the Adirondacks to squeeze into one chapter. It could take a lifetime to travel the hundreds of trails that wind through the wilderness. Nearby Keene Valley (located 19 miles east of Lake Placid on Route 73) is known as the "home of the High Peaks." It seems you can't throw a stone without hitting a trailhead and most trails are no less than spectacular. The trailhead for the highest of the 46 peaks, Mount Marcy, is in Keene Valley, as are numerous other well-known hikes. Following are several easily accessible hikes that start near the Village of Lake Placid. Guidebooks specifically geared to hiking are available in local bookstores and outdoor stores.

MT. JO HIKE

(Adirondak Loj Rd. ☎ 518.523.3441) The hike up Mt. Jo is a short 2.3-mile loop trail. The hike is considered "moderate" but offers fantastic views of the High Peaks from the open summit ledges. The hike begins at the Adirondak Loj, a popular hiking access point in the **Adirondack High Peaks Wilderness Area**. There is a parking fee, which is rare in the park, but the parking lot is run by the Adirondack Mountain Club.

The trailhead is located approximately eight miles south of Lake Placid. From Lake Placid, go three miles south on Route 73 toward Keene and Keene Valley. Turn right on Adirondak Loj Road at the High Peaks Trailhead sign. Continue five miles to the parking area. ($)

CASCADE MOUNTAIN

(Route 73) Cascade Mountain is the easiest of the 46 Peaks (those over 4,000 feet) to summit. The 4.8-mile (roundtrip) hike is considered "moderate" and rewards those who ascend with wonderful 360-degree views. The summit is rocky and open, and provides a great introduction to first-timers to the area. The trail is one of the most heavily traveled in the High Peaks, yet it is well preserved.

The trailhead is located off Route 73 between Lake Placid and Keene (8.5 miles south of Lake Placid). Coming from Lake Placid, there is a trail sign posted on the right side of the road with Cascade Mountain and Porter Mountain listed.

MT. VAN HOEVENBERG

(Route 73) Mt. Van Hoevenberg is a popular trail for hikers, runners and mountain bikers. The route is 4.4 miles roundtrip and is considered "moderate." The start of the trail is mostly level and meanders through the woods. After about a mile, the trail climbs a wooded hillside and gains approximately 1,800 feet to the summit. Views from open ledges along the way provide nice views of the High Peaks to the south including a view of Mount Marcy.

From Lake Placid, follow Route 73 south toward Keene Valley. After 3.5 miles, turn right onto Adirondak Loj Road. Continue 3.8 miles and turn left onto Meadows Lane. The trailhead parking lot is less than a half mile on the left.

MOUNT BAKER

(Saranac Lake) It is a two-mile round-trip hike to the summit of Mount Baker in Saranac Lake. The top offers wonderful views of the Saranac Lakes and the High Peaks through the trees. The hike is considered "easy," and the summit is approximately 2,450 feet. From downtown Saranac Lake on Main Street, go to Dugway. At the end of Dugway, take the first left onto Forest Hill Avenue. The trailhead is at Moody Pond. Parking is next to the pond across from the trailhead.

AMPERSAND MOUNTAIN

(Saranac Lake) Ampersand Mountain is a "moderate" hike of 5.4 miles roundtrip. Views from the bare summit are considered some of the best in the park and include the Saranac Lakes, Tupper Lake, and the High Peaks. The first mile or so of the hike is relatively flat but this changes abruptly for the ascent up the mountain. From Saranac Lake, take Route 3 west approximately eight miles. There is a parking area on the right. The trailhead is opposite the parking area (east side of the road).

MOUNTAIN BIKING

Mountain biking has gained popularity in the Adirondacks in recent years. Although mountain bikes are not permitted on trails in designated Primitive Areas and Wilderness Areas, they are allowed in Wild Forest areas. In Essex County, Wild Forest areas include Vanderwacker Mountain Wild Forest and Hammond Pond Wild Forest. There are also several other well-established mountain biking areas as described below.

OLYMPIC SPORTS COMPLEX

(220 Bob Run ☎ 518.523.8972 🖱 orda.org) During the summer season, the Olympic Sports Complex opens 30 miles of its cross-country ski trails to mountain biking. The terrain is mostly a combination of wide trails and single track, but there are also slalom courses and jumps. Trails are easy to follow and well marked with their level of difficulty. The Olympic Sports Complex is located at Mt. Van Hoevenberg. The entrance is on Route 73, southeast of the ski jumping complex. Follow the signs to the biathlon training center. The mountain bike center is on the right. There is a small store and repair shop operated by **High Peaks Cyclery** for bike rentals and essentials. Trail pass fees are nominal and mountain bikes are available for rent. ($)

WHITEFACE MOUNTAIN SKI CENTER

(5021 Route 86, Wilmington ☎ 518.946.2223
🖱 **whiteface.com/summer)** In recent years, mountain biking has taken off at **Whiteface Mountain**. The Whiteface Mountain Bike Park offers all levels of trails to downhill bikers via 27 different routes. Expert-only trails are reached from the

summit of Little Whiteface, which is accessed by lift service in the Cloudsplitter Gondola. Riders can expect rough terrain, tight turns and steep drops, as Whiteface is known for the greatest vertical drop in the east. One run alone can take between 30 and 45 minutes.

The park also offers shuttle service for beginner and intermediate bikers to a drop-off point with a nice selection of trails to traverse the lower mountain. The park also offers advanced cross-country trails. The Whiteface Mountain Bike Park is open from late June through early September. Trail maps are available online. Lessons are offered, and bikes and safety equipment are available for rent. ($)

WILMINGTON CROSS-COUNTRY TRAILS

(Rte 86, Wilmington) A three-mile network of trails is located off Route 86, north of the bridge by the Flume Falls in Wilmington. Visitors can park in the Flume Falls parking lot, and enjoy single track on cross-country ski trails and old roads near the Ausable River.

PINE POND

(Averyville Rd.) A seven-mile trail of hard-packed, double-track terrain begins at the end of Averyville Road in Lake Placid. The trail leads to a secluded kettle pond.

FOWLER'S CROSSING

(Rte 86, Saranac Lake) At Fowler's Crossing, where the railroad tracks cross Route 86, there is a four-mile network of trails called Fowler's Crossing Trail Network. Visitors can park at the Route 86 crossing parking lot and head either north or south of the road. The trail network is a series of loops and spurs. From Lake Placid, head west on Route 86 (toward Saranac Lake) until the road crosses the railroad tracks.

BLOOMINGDALE BOG

(Rte 86, Saranac Lake) The eight-mile Bloomingdale Bog trail is located just north of Saranac Lake off Route 86. An old right-of-way for the railroad offers easy access to the bog. The trail is a combination of sand, dirt and gravel with some roots along the way. The scenery is beautiful, as the trail overlooks the mountains. This trail is also a favorite of bird watchers.

PADDLE SPORTS

It is hard to find a location that rivals that of the Adirondacks for canoeing, kayaking and rafting. Hundreds of miles of canoe trails traverse the park and it could take a lifetime to explore all of them.

There is a large paddling community in the Lake Placid area. Many canoe and kayak races are held in the Adirondacks each year that draw competitors from around the world. Sprint competitions are held on Mirror Lake and endurance paddling events, such as the well-known Adirondack Canoe Classic (a 90-mile race) are held on nearby rivers and lakes.

There are many outfitters that rent canoes and kayaks and also provide guided trips. There is also white water rafting not far from Lake Placid.

ADIRONDACK LAKES & TRAILS

(Saranac Lake ☎ 800.491.0414 🩳 adirondackoutfitters.com)
Adirondack Lakes & Trails is a full-service canoe and kayak outfitter offering sales, rentals and guided instruction. They sell canoes, kayaks, outdoor clothing and gear. ($/$$)

ADIRONDACK RAFTING COMPANY

(☎ 518.523.1635 🩳 lakeplacidrafting.com) Adirondack Rafting Company runs white water rafting trips from April to October on the Hudson River Gorge near Indian Lake. Rapids classes range from III to V, depending on the weather and time of year. Indian Lake is about 73 miles southwest of Lake Placid (about a 1.75-hour drive each way). ($$)

MAC'S CANOE LIVERY

(5859 State Rte 30, Lake Clear ☎ 518.891.1176
🩳 **macscanoe.com)** Mac's Canoe is a family-owned-and-operated canoe livery offering rentals, sales, guided trips and shuttle service. They also host a series of canoe and kayak races through the Adirondack Watershed Alliance (an organization formed to assure the continued promotion and organization of paddlesport activities). Mac's is located near the St. Regis Canoe Area, approximately 20 miles from Lake Placid. The owners/guides are friendly, professional and knowledgeable about the area, and make sure that each guest gets the most out of their paddling experience. ($/$$)

MIDDLE EARTH EXPEDITIONS

(☎ 518.523.7172 🩳 adirondackrafting.com) Middle Earth Expeditions offers white water rafting and guided canoe trips on the Hudson River. Trips run from Indian Lake, and rapids classes range from III to V, depending on the weather and time of year. Middle Earth Expeditions specialize in providing personalized attention to small groups. Indian Lake is about 73 miles southwest of Lake Placid (about a 1.75-hour drive each way). ($$)

ST. REGIS CANOE OUTFITTERS

(73 Dorsey St. Saranac Lake ☎ 518.891.1838 ⬤ canoeoutfitters.com) St. Regis Canoe Outfitters is a full-service canoe and kayak outfitter based in Saranac Lake. They offer equipment sales, boat rentals, guided paddling trips, trip planning, shuttle transportation, private guiding and food packing for outdoor trips. They also sell outdoor equipment online and in their store. They have a second base located in Lake Clear. ($/$$)

WHITEFACE MOUNTAIN

Visitors won't be disappointed with a trip up **Whiteface Mountain** and **Little Whiteface Mountain**. The views from both are spectacular—and getting there is half the fun!

LITTLE WHITEFACE MOUNTAIN

(☎ 518.946.2223 ⬤ whiteface.com) Little Whiteface Mountain is where the ski resort currently operates. In the summer, the Cloudsplitter Gondola is open for sight-seeing rides up the mountain. From the top, Lake Placid, the ski jumps, the Ausable River and the High Peaks can be viewed as well as Lake Champlain on a clear day. Nature treks are available at the base of the mountain and include a hike, lunch and gondola ride. Disc golf is also offered. ($/$$)

WHITEFACE MOUNTAIN/VETERANS MEMORIAL HWY

(Wilmington ☎ 518.946.2223) At 4,867 feet, Whiteface Mountain is the fifth-highest peak in New York State. There are several ways to enjoy the mountain and the spectacular 360-degree view from the top. As one of the 46 Peaks, hiking is a popular option. The shortest trail up begins west of Wilmington and ascends approximately 3,600 feet in just over five miles. A round-trip hike takes on average, about seven hours. If hiking isn't your thing, you can still enjoy the spectacular views by driving the Whiteface Veterans Memorial Highway.

The highway is eight miles long and winds around the north side of the mountain. There are nine scenic overlooks. At the end of the road is a small stone castle, a restaurant, gift shop and parking lot. The summit is a fifth of a mile higher and can be accessed either by hiking trail or by an elevator that was carved into solid rock. This toll route is open (weather permitting) from May through October. Road bikes are also permitted to tackle the highway descent for a small fee. ($)

HORSEBACK RIDING

Experiencing the Adirondacks from the back of a horse can be a fun and inspiring way to connect with nature. There are several local stables that offer guided trail rides.

ADIRONDACK EQUINE CENTER

(Rte 86 ☎ 518.834.9933
☗ adirondackequinecenter.com/sleigh.html) The Adirondack Equine Center offers guided trail rides in Lake Placid. Each

ride is led by a knowledgeable guide who leads the group on the trail, assists riders and answers questions. An orientation lesson is given prior to the ride to teach guests the basics of horsemanship and safety. ($/$$)

EMERALD SPRINGS RANCH

(651 Rte 186, Saranac Lake ☎ 518.891.3727) Emerald Springs Ranch is a small quarter horse ranch located near the Village of Saranac Lake. They specialize in taking small family groups for trail rides. Children are welcome, and rides take place rain or shine. The ranch is open all year. Accommodations are also available on site. ($/$$)

SCENIC RAILROAD RIDES

Scenic Railroad rides on the historic Adirondack Scenic Railroad can be a treat for people of all ages. Wonderfully restored railroad cars are used for these short, informative rides.

ADIRONDACK SCENIC RAILROAD

(20 Averyville Rd. ☎ 518.523.4237) Visitors can ride the rails between Lake Placid and Saranac Lake on the historic Adirondack Scenic Railroad. Depart from either Lake Placid Station or Saranac Lake Union Depot and ride 20 miles round trip. The ride is 45 minutes each way with a 45-minute layover. ($/$$)

ADIRONDACK SCENIC RAILROAD RAIL & CANOE

(St. Regis Canoe Outfitters, 73 Dorsey St. Saranac Lake ☎ 518.891.1838 ⬥ canoeoutfitters.com) Visitors can ride the Adirondack Scenic Railroad from Lake Placid to Saranac Lake, then paddle the Saranac River in a canoe or kayak. Paddlers are then transported back to the Saranac Lake Depot for the rail ride back to Lake Placid. ($/$$)

TENNIS

Many hotels and resorts offer the use of private tennis courts to their guests. There are also a few public courts available in and around the village. There are public tennis courts available just off Main Street by the Toboggan Chute. Parking is available on the street. In Saranac Lake, there are free, lighted, public tennis courts adjacent to Lake Flower (by the Sara-Placid Motor Inn) on Route 86. The courts are located in a small public park.

OTHER SUMMER ACTIVITIES

There is always something to discover during summers in Lake Placid.

CROSS COUNTRY BIATHLON CENTER

(Olympic Sports Complex, 220 Bob Run, Rte 73
☎ **518.523.2811 🖱 whiteface.com)** Cross-country skiing and shooting may seem like an odd combination, but biathlon's roots as a training exercise for soldiers in Norway may help visitors understand the motivation behind the event. The Olympic Sports Complex offers the opportunity to try biathlon during the summer months. Professional instructors lead students through the process using .22 caliber rifles and targets used in the 1998 Nagano Winter Olympics. ($$)

HUNTING, ADIRONDACK FOOTHILLS GUIDE SERVICE

(Saranac Lake ☎ 518.359.8194 ☗ adkfoothills.com) Hunting is a popular sport in the Adirondacks. Common takes are duck, wild turkey, deer, and bear. Hunting season dates can be found on the New York State Department of Environmental Conservation website (dec.ny.gov). Hunting licenses can be obtained from the Town Clerk on Main Street.

Adirondack Foothills Guide Service offers guided hunting trips in a nonagricultural forest area. They hunt in challenging wilderness and wild lands. The business was established in 1982 and is family owned and operated.

SUMMER ICE SKATING (OLYMPIC CENTER)

(2634 Main St. ☎ 518.523.1655 ☗ whiteface.com) Ice skating is far from just a winter activity in Lake Placid. Professional skaters come from all over the world to live and train in Lake Placid, and visitors can share some of their ice in the summer and winter.

Public ice skating is allowed in the USA Rink in the Olympic Center during the summer months. A public skating schedule is posted online on the weekly calendar of events. ($)

Winter Activities

Winter brings a whole new landscape and a distinct new group of visitors to Lake Placid. The Adirondacks is a rare destination where summer and winter activities rival one another in popularity. As snow blankets the mountains and lakes freeze over, winter sports enthusiasts wax their skis, sharpen their skating blades and polish their snowmobiles. The smell of woodstoves floats through the air and rosy-cheeked people walk the streets in brightly colored hats and snow boots. Pub lights come on early and wood burning fireplaces replace outdoor patios as the evening gathering place. These are all sure signs that winter recreation has come to Lake Placid, and the town barely skips a beat in its transition.

CROSS-COUNTRY SKIING

Cross-country skiing is available in several locations around Lake Placid. Seemingly endless wilderness lends itself extremely well to this quiet yet challenging sport.

CASCADES CROSS-COUNTRY SKI CENTER
(Rte 73 ☎ 518.523.1111 🖰 cascadeski.com) The Cascades Cross-Country Ski Center is a full-service cross-country ski facility offering sales, rentals, lessons, lodging, restaurant, bar and 20 kilometers of groomed trails. Located on Route 73, just five miles east of Lake Placid, their trail systems connect with those of Mt. Van Hoevenberg and the Jack Rabbit trail. Their staff is friendly and knowledgeable, and their full moon parties are legendary. ($)

OLYMPIC SPORTS COMPLEX

(220 Bob Run, Rte 73 ☎ 518.523.2811 ◉ whiteface.com) The Olympic Sports Complex at Mt. Van Hoevenberg provides beautiful cross-country ski terrain for all levels of skiers. The facility offers equipment rentals, lessons, a ski shop and café. A facility schedule, ski conditions, trail maps, rates and season pass information can be found online. ($)

JACKRABBIT TRAIL

(Adirondack Ski Touring Council ☎ 518.523.1365) The Jackrabbit Trail was developed by the Adirondack Ski Touring Council (ASTC) with the intent of promoting cross-country skiing in Lake Placid and the surrounding area. It is named after a skiing pioneer in Lake Placid, Herman "Jackrabbit" Johannsen, a native Norwegian who lived to be 111. The trail is currently more than 35 miles long and an ongoing improvement schedule is in place. The trail can be accessed at various points in Lake Placid, Saranac Lake and Ray Brook. Trail maps are available in the village or can be obtained from the ASTC.

WILMINGTON CROSS-COUNTRY TRAILS

(Rte 86, Wilmington) A three-mile network of trails is located off Route 86, north of the bridge by the Flume Falls in Wilmington. Visitors can park in the Flume Falls parking lot, and enjoy a combination of cross-country ski trails and old roads near the Ausable River.

DOG SLEDDING ✪ Must See!

During the Olympics in 1932, 13 mushers competed in a 22.5-mile derby around Lake Placid that started and ended in the Olympic Arena. Ever since, dog sledding has been a part of

Lake Placid's resume. Now two tour companies offer visitors the chance to learn about the sport and ride with their sled dogs.

THUNDER MOUNTAIN DOG SLED TOURS

(Mirror Lake ☎ 518.891.6239) Thunder Mountain Dog Sled Tours offers dog sled rides on Mirror Lake in the village. They are based in Vermontville, New York, but they can easily be found on Mirror Lake most weekends in the winter (once the lake is frozen) in front of the **Mirror Lake Inn**. Guests can learn about dog sledding and test it out on a short ride across the lake. Those interested in learning more and taking a longer trip can schedule a wilderness ride through the woods. Riders should dress in warm clothes and be prepared for a breeze! ($)

GOLDEN ARROW DOGSLEDS

(Golden Arrow Lakeside Resort and Suites, 2559 Main St.
☎ 518.523.3353) For over 30 years, a family team has offered dog sled rides in front of the **Golden Arrow Lakeside Resort** on Mirror Lake. The father-and-son mushing team conducts tours on most weekends and additional days during the week (weather permitting). The family owns about 25 Alaskan huskies, which are bred for the cold weather and endurance. ($)

DOWNHILL SKIING AND SNOWBOARDING

Downhill skiing and snowboarding are the primary reason many people come to Lake Placid in the winter. Whiteface is the most popular downhill resort in the area. It is located in nearby Wilmington and was the site of the downhill Olympic events. There are also several other ski areas within a reasonable driving distance for a day trip. The ski resorts rent equipment on site, but there are sports shops in town that also rent and sell equipment.

CUNNINGHAM'S SKI BARN

(109 Main St. ☎ 518.523.3706 ⬤ cunninghamsskibarn.com)
Cunninghan's Ski Barn, located on Main Street, is a full-service ski and snowboard shop. They sell and rent alpine skis, snowboards, and backcountry and cross-country ski equipment. They also offer apparel and have a repair shop.

GORE MOUNTAIN

(Peaceful Valley Rd., North Creek ☎ 518.251.2411
⬤ goremountain.com) Gore Mountain is located in North Creek, New York, approximately a 1.5-hour drive from Lake Placid. The resort offers 88 alpine and glade trails and 2,300 vertical feet. The resort has eight lifts, including a high-speed quad, a gondola and a high-speed triple. Upgrades and expansions to the resort are made annually. ($$/$$$)

MAUI NORTH

(134 Main St. ☎ 518.523.7245 ⬤ mauinorth.net) Maui North specializes in skis, snowboards and sports apparel. Their knowledgeable staff and owner have been testing equipment for manufacturers for more than 25 years. The store prides itself in offering the technical knowledge to best assist their customers. Maui North also offers rentals and a second store in Plattsburgh, New York.

MT. PISGAH SKI CENTER

(Mt. Pisgah Rd., Saranac Lake ☎ 518.891.0970
⬤ saranaclakeny.gov) Mt. Pisgah is a cozy little ski area in the Village of Saranac Lake, with five ski runs, a snowboarding terrain park and a two-lane tubing hill. It has 320 feet of vertical on 15 acres. The ski area receives an average of seven feet of snow per year. Mt. Pisgah is wonderful for families and

offers lessons through a local ski club. They also offer night skiing. ($)

TITUS MOUNTAIN
(215 Johnson Rd. Malone ☎ 518.483.3740
☗ **titusmountain.com)** Titus Mountain is located 52 miles north-northwest of Lake Placid. It is a great ski resort for beginner and intermediate downhillers, and is normally not very crowded. There are 27 trails and 1,200 vertical feet. This is a family mountain with very reasonable lift pass and rental prices. ($$)

WHITEFACE SKI RESORT
(5021 Rte 86, Wilmington ☎ 518.946.2223
☗ **whiteface.com)** Whiteface Mountain is the primary downhill ski resort near Lake Placid. It boasts the greatest vertical drop (over 3,400 feet) east of the Rocky Mountains. Whiteface has also been ranked number one in *Ski* magazine among eastern United States skiing and snowboarding resorts.

Updates to Whiteface are always in the works. New trails, new lifts and new snowmaking capabilities are a few of the ongoing projects at the resort. The resort offers 86 trails and the longest run is more than two miles. The average annual snowfall is 230 inches.

For non-skiing visitors, gondola rides in the Cloudsplitter Gondola are available for a small fee or as part of the Olympic Sites Passport. Be prepared to share the ride with skiers if you have less than four in your party. ($$/$$$)

HOCKEY AND SKATING

Public skating is available all year in Lake Placid at the **Olympic Center**. In the winter the **Sheffield Speed Skating Oval** is open to the public during certain hours. and there is also skating on Mirror Lake.

HOCKEY PLUS LAKE PLACID

(2663 Main St. ☎ 518.523.4254 ☋ lakeplacidhockeyplus.com)
The Hockey Plus on Main Street sells hockey equipment, team gear, bags, accessories, apparel and collectibles. Located across from the speed skating oval and the Olympic Center, it is easily accessible to the hockey rinks and surrounding hotels.

LAKE PLACID SKATE SHOP

(6197 Sentinel Rd. ☎ 518.523.0229 ☋ lakeplacidskates.com)
The Lake Placid Skate Shop offers equipment and apparel for speed skating and figure skating. They also sell skating memorabilia, photographs and artwork. Their motto is "Live. Love. Skate" and the friendly owners seem committed to doing just that.

PUBLIC ICE SKATING

(Olympic Center, 2634 Main St. ☎ 518.523.1655
☋ **whiteface.com)** Public ice skating is offered at the **Olympic Center** in two rinks. One rink is inside the Olympic Center building and the other is the **Sheffield Speed Skating Oval** just outside the Olympic Center (during the winter only). A public skating schedule is posted online on the weekly calendar of events. Tickets are inexpensive and on-site rentals are available. ($)

SNOWMOBILING

Snowmobiling is a favorite winter sport in the Adirondacks, and the park is known as a premier destination for riding. Hundreds of miles of groomed and backcountry trails are easily accessible, and riders can skim the deep snow through forests, over mountains and through quaint towns that offer warm and cozy after-ride accommodations. Lake Placid is no exception, and those wishing to rent snowmobiles or to try the sport for the first time can do so easily.

LAKE PLACID SNOWMOBILING, INC.

(Main St. ☎ 518.523.3596 ◔ lakeplacidsnowmobiling.com) Lake Placid Snowmobiling, Inc., offers snowmobile rides on a 12-mile trail through pine forests and Christmas tree farms. They use modern equipment, and run tours daily in winter—longer tours can be arranged. The company has been in business for more than 15 years. Thumb and hand warmers are provided. They also cater to groups. ($$)

FARMHOUSE SNOWMOBILING

(129 Hobart Rd., Paul Smiths ☎ 518.327.3429 ◔ adirondacks.com/farmhouse_snowmobiling) Farmhouse Snowmobiling welcomes experienced and first-time riders for guided snowmobile tours. With direct access to a large trail system, they take guests through forests, over fields and on the state snowmobile trails. Tours are kept small to allow for personalization. Helmets and hand warmers are provided. Reservations are required. ($$)

SNOW TOURS, INC.

(☎ 518.523.3415 ◔ adirondacks.com/snowtours) Snow Tours, Inc., offers snowmobile tours from one to six hours in length.

They accommodate both beginner and advanced riders, and have single and double snowmobiles with backrests. Snow Tours, Inc., offers scenic rides, night tours and "aggressive" adventures for experienced riders. ($$)

OTHER WINTER ACTIVITIES

A wide range of winter activites are available throughout the Lake Placid area, particularly at the **Olympic Sports Complex** and the **Whiteface Mountain** area. This section details some of the more exotic winter recreation activities.

BOBSLEDDING ✪ Must See!
(Olympic Sports Complex, 220 Bob Run, Rte 73
☎ **518.523.4436** 🖱 **whiteface.com)** It is difficult to describe a bobsled ride. Hair-raising acceleration, steeply banked turns and barely time to breathe are the first things that come to mind. The **Olympic Sports Complex** at Mt. Van Hoevenberg offers bobsled rides to the public. The ride begins at the half-mile mark on a competition track. The price may seem steep for a quick half-mile ride but it's an experience to remember. Rides are provided in four-person sleds, but can accommo-date two passengers per trip since a professional driver and brakeman operate the sled. Wait times can be long in the height of the winter season, and there is a minimum height require-ment of 48 inches. ($$/$$$)

CROSS COUNTRY BIATHLON CENTER
(Olympic Sports Complex, 220 Bob Run, Rte 73
☎ **518.523.2811** 🖱 **whiteface.com)** Visitors may wonder what cross-country skiing and rifle shooting have in common, but it makes perfect sense when they learn that the sport of

biathlon began as a training exercise for soldiers in Norway. This Scandinavian sport is only taught in a few places, and the Olympic Sports Complex in Lake Placid is one of them. Hour-long lessons include a freestyle ski lesson followed by a trip to the on-site firing range. Students are under the careful supervision of experienced instructors as they learn about this unique sport. Visitors can also choose to participate just in the firing range portion if desired. Check the activities calendar online for available times, or call for additional information and rates. ($$)

GONDOLA RIDES (WHITEFACE SKI AREA)
(5021 Rte 86, Wilmington ☎ 518.946.2223

☗ whiteface.com) Skiers aren't the only people who can enjoy views from the top of **Little Whiteface Mountain**. Visitors wishing to get a bird's-eye view of the Adirondacks can ride the eight-person Cloudsplitter Gondola from the base lodge to the top of Little Whiteface. The 15-minute ride goes over forests, steep rock formations, streams and ski trails. From the top, the view is stunning. The Village of Lake Placid, Lake Placid itself, the ski jumps, Ausable River and, on a clear day, Lake Champlain, are all in view. There is an observation deck and picnic area from which to enjoy the view. ($/$$)

SKELETON (OLYMPIC SPORTS COMPLEX)
(220 Bob Run, Rte 73 ☎ 518.523.4436 ☗ whiteface.com) Lake
Placid offers the rare opportunity to try the sport of skeleton. Visitors unfamiliar with the skeleton may be amazed and/or terrified at the site of this sport. It appears to be a children's sled on steroids as drivers lie on their stomachs and blast down a chute of ice at 30 miles per hour. Visitors can try the skeleton at the Olympic Sports Complex on the competition track. The

course is open for public rides most Saturdays and holiday weeks, depending on weather, track conditions and competition schedules. Rates are slightly less than the cost of a bobsled ride and the minimum age is 13. Call ahead for reservations. ($$/$$$)

SNOWSHOEING (OLYMPIC SPORTS COMPLEX)

(220 Bob Run, Rte 73 ☎ 518.523.2811 ☗ whiteface.com) Trails for snowshoeing are available in multiple locations near Lake Placid. Visitors who like to hike—but prefer shoes over skates or skis—may enjoy taking to the trails on snowshoes. The **Olympic Sports Complex** offers miles of snowshoe trails through the beautiful Adirondack woods. Daily and multi-day passes are available. Rental equipment is also available. Check online for trail maps and facility schedules. Discounts are available for seniors and students. ($)

LAKE PLACID TOBOGGAN CHUTE

(Parkside Dr. ☎ 518.523.2591 ☗ northelba.org) Where else but in a winter sports playground such as Lake Placid can visitors enjoy a massive toboggan chute right in the middle of town? Once the ice thickens on Mirror Lake, the Lake Placid Toboggan Chute opens for business. Children of all ages can enjoy riding toboggans down a 30-foot-high converted ski jump trestle onto the lake and see how far they can slide on the ice. Sleds hold two to four people, and tickets allow multiple rides during a specific time period.

The Toboggan Chute opened in the 1960s and is currently operated by the North Elba Park District. Since operation is dependent on ice conditions, opening and closing days vary each year. Expect a wait during busy holiday times although hours are often extended during peak times. ($)

Sporting Events

There is no shortage of sporting events in Lake Placid. Year-round, visitors can enjoy a wide variety of spectator and participatory sports. The well-maintained Olympic venues host world-class winter competitions, and it is not uncommon to see international athletes with their team jackets walking around town. Bobsled teams, figure skaters, skiers, lugers, hockey teams and biathletes are just some of the athletes who train and compete in Lake Placid.

Likewise, world-class summer events have migrated to Lake Placid. The arrival of **Ironman USA** triggered an onslaught of triathletes to the area, and throughout much of the year, people train for the swim, bike and run on the Ironman course. Many other sports shape the summer landscape of the village. There are horse shows, rowing competitions, mountain bike races and fishing tournaments, to name a few.

Lake Placid could easily be called the sports capital of the East. The combination of natural and manmade venues, and the draw of the natural beauty of the area make it an enticing location for competitors to travel to. Armchair sports fans won't be disappointed either, as many of the events are held either in the village or close to the village, and entrance to the events is normally quick, often free and always easily accessible.

SPRING EVENTS

Even before the ice melts, fishing events begin in the Adirondacks. Once the ice is gone, a whole new world of activities awakens for the season.

COLBY CLASSIC ICE FISHING DERBY

(Colby Lake, Saranac Lake ☎ 518.891.2560) The Saranac Lake Fish and Game Club hosts an annual ice fishing derby at the beginning of March. The tournament is held on Lake Colby in Saranac Lake (on Route 86).

AUSABLE RIVER TWO-FLY CHALLENGE

(West Branch Ausable River, Wilmington
⊖ whitefaceregion.com/fishtwoflycontest.cfm) The Ausable River Two-Fly Challenge is an annual fly-fishing contest that takes place in May in Wilmington. Each angler chooses two barbless flies. Participants can angle for up to 10 hours or until both flies are unusable. The event is catch-and-release, and there is a dinner, awards ceremony and guest speaker after the event.

ROUND THE MOUNTAIN CANOE AND KAYAK RACES

(Adirondack Watershed Alliance, Lake Clear ☎ 518.891.2744
⊖ macscanoe.com) The Round the Mountain Canoe and Kayak Races are held each May in Saranac Lake. The race course begins on Lower Saranac Lake and ends 10.5 miles later on Lake Flower in the Village of Saranac Lake.

SUMMER EVENTS

Lake Placid hosts back-to-back sporting events in the summer. A wide variety of sports challenges make their way to the village—and with them come athletes, spectators and vendors.

NYSEF OPEN GOLF TOURNAMENT

(Lake Placid Club Mountain Golf Course ☎ 518.946.7001
⊖ nysef.org) The Lake Placid Club hosts an annual golf tour-

nament in June to benefit the New York Ski Educational Foundation. The tournament is played on the Lake Placid Club Mountain Course in teams of four. Players can enter individually or as a team. All funds generated by the event benefit local and statewide winter sports athletes.

WHITEFACE MOUNTAIN UPHILL BIKE RACE

(Whiteface Mountain Veterans Memorial Hwy, Wilmington ☎ 518.946.2255 👆 whitefacerace.com) The annual Whiteface Mountain Uphill Bike Race offers a challenging eight-mile ride up Whiteface Mountain on the Whiteface Mountain Veterans Memorial Highway. The ascent is 3,500 feet. Participants are rewarded with a panoramic view of the Adirondacks, extending into Canada and New England. The event is held each June and is sponsored by the Whiteface Mountain Regional Visitors Bureau. The start line is at the intersection of Routes 86 and 431 in Wilmington.

WHITEFACE MOUNTAIN UPHILL FOOT RACE

(Whiteface Mountain Veterans Memorial Hwy, Wilmington ☎ 518.946.2255 👆 whitefacerace.com) The annual Whiteface Mountain Uphill Foot Race has a history of more than 30 years. The scenic 3,500-foot climb up the Whiteface Mountain Veterans Memorial Highway brings participants to the top of the fifth-highest peak in the Adirondacks. Like the uphill bike races, the course is eight miles long with an average 8% grade. The race is sponsored by the Whiteface Mountain Regional Visitors Bureau.

LAKE PLACID MARATHON & HALF MARATHON

(1936 Saranac Ave., Ste 2-257 ⬤ lakeplacidmarathon.com) Each June, the Lake Placid Marathon & Half Marathon is held in the village. The start for both races is on Main Street in front of the **Sheffield Speed Skating Oval.** Approximately 2,500 people participate and the event has a mass start. Finishers' medals are awarded to finishers in both races in addition to top-finisher awards.

LAKE PLACID SUMMER FIGURE SKATING CHAMPIONSHIPS

(Olympic Center, 2634 Main St. ☎ 518.523.1655 ⬤ lakeplacidskating.com) The annual Lake Placid Summer Figure Skating Championships is held at the **Olympic Center** in June. The event is hosted by the Skating Club of Lake Placid and the New York State Olympic Regional Development Authority. Skaters can enter the short program and/or free skating competition. Seminars are provided at no additional charge to participating skaters and coaches. The event is sanctioned by U.S. Figure Skating and Skate Canada.

TUPPER LAKE 9-MILER

(Adirondack Watershed Alliance, Lake Clear ☎ 518.891.2744 ⬤ macscanoe.com) The Tupper Lake 9-Miler is a nine-mile paddling race in Tupper Lake. The race is held in June and is normally a point-to-point. There are a number of divisions for canoes, kayaks and guide boats.

LAKE PLACID HORSE SHOW

(The Lake Placid Horse Show Association, 5514 Cascade Rd. ☎ 518.523.9625 ⬤ lakeplacidhorseshow.com) Each year, hundreds of horses and riders from across the country descend on the beautiful North Elba Show Grounds for the Lake Placid Horse Show and I Love New York Horse Show. The Lake Placid Horse Show has been held for more than 40 years, and the I Love New York Horse Show has been held for over 30 years. The show grounds are the perfect location for such a big event. They sit in the shadows of the Olympic ski jumps and have a backdrop of Whiteface Mountain.

The shows are scheduled annually back to back during the last week in June and first week in July. World-class horses and riders compete in hunter and jumper competitions, and more than $450,000 in prize money is awarded. Spectator tickets can be purchased for a nominal fee.

IRONMAN USA

(🖰 ironmanlakeplacid.com) It is difficult not to be impressed by athletes competing in an ultra-distance triathlon. Ironman USA is one of the best-known triathlon events in the country, and Lake Placid is an amazing venue for this brutal competition. Athletes race through a 2.4-mile swim, a 112-mile road bike ride and then run a marathon (26.2 miles)—all in a single day. More than 2,500 athletes converge on the village once a year in late July for this incredible endurance event. They have 17 hours to cross the finish line, which is set up on the **Sheffield Speed Skating Oval**. Spectating for this event is an endurance activity in itself, but one to be remembered as fans encourage their favorite athletes and total strangers across the finish line.

LAKE PLACID INTERNATIONAL CANOE & KAYAK REGATTA

(Mirror Lake 🌢 lakeplacidinternational.com) The Lake Placid International Canoe & Kayak Regatta is held annually over the first weekend in July on Mirror Lake. World-class sprint canoe and kayak competitors compete in numerous divisions throughout the weekend. Races start from the **Mirror Lake Beach.**

SUNDOWNER SERIES

(Adirondack Watershed Alliance, Lake Clear ☎ 518.891.2744 🌢 macscanoe.com) The Sundowner Series is held each summer on every other Tuesday at the Saranac Inn state boat launch on Upper Saranac Lake. The series offers paddlers the chance to participate in clinics and time trials on the lake. Informal clinics include everything from paddling strokes to wake riding. Dates and times are posted on the event website.

CAN/AM RUGBY TOURNAMENT

(P.O. Box 774, Saranac Lake 🌢 canamrugby.com) The annual CAN/AM Rugby Tournament is the largest rugby tournament in North America. It is held at the end of July or early August in Saranac Lake and Lake Placid. The tournament was started by the Mountaineers Rugby Club of Saranac Lake in 1974 and blossomed from an eight-team competition into the current 100-plus team tournament. Spectator admission is free.

XTERRA LAKE PLACID

(☎ 808.521.4322 🌢 xterraplanet.com) The XTERRA Lake Placid off-road triathlon is a relatively new event to the village, debuting in 2009. Athletes are tested in a 1,500-meter swim in

Mirror Lake, followed by a 25K mountain bike ride and a 10K run. The race is held the third weekend in August. Transitions are held on the **Sheffield Speed Skating Oval** in front of the Lake Placid High School.

LAKE PLACID SUMMIT LACROSSE TOURNAMENT

(North Elba Athletic Fields 🖰 lakeplacidlax.com) The Lake Placid Summit Lacrosse Tournament is held annually in August at the North Elba Athletic fields. The tournament has more than a 20-year history and is the largest of its kind in North America. This is a family event with a large variety of divisions. Upward of 90 teams enter the event each year from both the United States and Canada.

PAT STRATTON MEMORIAL BICYCLE RIDE

(Mt. Pisgah, Saranac Lake 🖰 bikeadirondacks.org) The annual Pat Stratton Memorial Bicycle Ride is held at the end of August. The event includes a century ride (100 miles), 50-mile ride, 25-mile ride, and a kids' ride. All routes are well supported and there's a barbeque following the ride. Proceeds from the ride benefit the Saranac Lake Kiwanis Club.

FALL EVENTS

There is no slowdown of activity come fall. Bike races and paddling events are just some of the fun competitions that attract athletes to the Village of Lake Placid in the fall.

WHITEFACE MOUNTAIN HILL CLIMB BIKE RACE

(Whiteface Mountain Veterans Memorial Highway, Wilmington ☎ 518.946.7001 🖰 nysef.org) Like the Whiteface Mountain

Uphill Bike Race, the annual Whiteface Mountain Hill Climb Bike Race is a grueling eight-mile uphill race on the Whiteface Mountain Veterans Memorial Highway. The course has an average grade of 8% and finishes at an altitude above 4,000 feet. The race is held in September and benefits the New York Ski Educational Foundation.

5K DOWNHILL MOUNTAIN BIKE RACE

(Whiteface Mountain Bike Park, Wilmington ☎ 518.946.2223 🖱 downhillmike.com) The annual 5K Downhill Mountain Bike Race is held at the Whiteface Mountain Ski Center in Wilmington. The race takes place in mid-September and is part of the Gravity East Series. Both amateurs and pros can compete in the race, and pros usually race for a substantial prize purse.

ADIRONDACK 540 BIKE RACE

(☎ 518.583.3708 🖱 adkultracycling.com/adk540) The Adirondack 540 is weekend-long ultra cycling event held annually in September. The course is 136 miles along Lake Champlain, through the High Peaks, and through Lake Placid.

ADIRONDACK CANOE CLASSIC

(Adirondack Watershed Alliance, Lake Clear ☎ 518.891.2744 🖱 macscanoe.com) The Adirondack Canoe Classic ("90-Miler") has a long history as the ultimate paddling challenge in the Adirondacks. Hosted by the Adirondack Watershed Alliance and **Mac's Canoe Livery**, the event is a three-day, 90-mile paddling race held each September. The race is on flat water, and is a combination of river and lake paddling with multiple carries. Participants enter numerous paddle craft divisions with canoes, kayaks, war canoes and guide boats. The race starts in Old Forge and ends in Saranac Lake.

LONG LAKE LONG BOAT REGATTA

(Adirondack Watershed Alliance, Lake Clear ☎ 518.891.2744 ⛵ macscanoe.com) The Long Lake Long Boat Regatta is held annually at the end of September. There are two courses, a 10-mile course and a 15-mile course. The race features a number of divisions and is host to the North American War Canoe Championships. All races begin in Long Lake at the beach across from the Adirondack Hotel.

Sporting Events

WINTER EVENTS

Winter sees a flood of world-class sporting events at all the Olympic venues and in other areas near the village. Athletes and spectators enjoy Lake Placid in the winter months as much as in the summer.

NEW YEAR'S MASTERS SKI JUMP COMPETITION

(Olympic Jumping Complex, 5486 Cascade Rd. ☎ 518.523.2202 ⛵ whiteface.com) Visitors can enjoy some of the nation's best ski jump and Nordic combined competition at the annual New Year's Masters Ski Jump Competition. Athletes compete for the Art Devlin Cup in three events with a history of more than 50 years. First the ski jumpers face off on the 90-meter jump at the **Olympic Jumping Complex**, after which the Nordic athletes move to the Olympic Sports Complex for the cross-country portion of the event.

LAKE PLACID LOPPET

(Olympic Sports Complex, 220 Bob Run, Rte 73
lakeplacidloppet.com) The Lake Placid Loppet is known as
one of the best annual cross-country ski events in the country.
For more than 25 years, thousands of skiers have raced the
trails at the Olympic Sports Complex at Mt. Van Hoevenberg.
The race includes a 50-kilometer course (30.1 miles) and a
25-kilometer course (15 miles). The race is open to skiers of
all levels, although the courses are demanding. The Lake Placid
Loppet is held in early February and is part of the American
Ski Marathon Series.

EMPIRE STATE WINTER GAMES

(empirestategames.org/winter) For more than 30 years, the
Empire State Winter Games have been held for events such as
skiing, biathlon, bobsled, figure skating, hockey, luge, skeleton,
speed skating, ski jumping and snowshoeing. The games are
held in Lake Placid for three days at the end of February. The
games are a program of the New York State Office of Parks,
Recreation and Historical Preservation but they are supported
by ORDA.

Lake George

The Town of Lake George, located in the southeastern portion of the Adirondacks in Warren County (two hours by car from Lake Placid), is another popular tourist destination in upstate New York. The town is named after Lake George, which borders the town at its most southern point.

Lake George is the largest lake in the Adirondacks. It is 30 miles long and three miles wide at its widest part. Although not a wide lake, it reaches depths of up to 200 feet.

The Town of Lake George has been a popular summer destination for decades. Lake George Village (located within the town), in particular, is the center of tourist activity. Although the village is surrounded by the Adirondack Mountains, it has a much different feel from the Village of Lake Placid. Lake George Village is more akin to a beach resort community, with a bustling main strip complete with shops, restaurants and motels next to a large public beach.

Lake George Village is convenient to many major East Coast cities. It is less than a four-hour drive from both New York City and Boston, and is a three-hour drive from Hartford, Connecticut.

SUMMER ACTIVITIES

Summer is prime season in Lake George. It offers visitors many choices for recreation and entertainment. Outdoor activities such as boating, fishing, hiking, horseback riding and golfing are convenient to Lake George Village, as is shopping and amusement parks. Special events are scheduled throughout the summer, and weekly fireworks displays can be seen on Thursdays in July and August.

WINTER IN LAKE GEORGE

Although Lake George is primarily a summer destination, a handful of winter activities and events take place in and around Lake George Village during the quiet months. Ice skating, snowmobiling and snowshoeing are some of the winter sports enjoyed in the area. The well-known **Winter Carnival** is also a 50-year tradition in Lake George.

Many establishments close during the winter months, so visitors should call ahead before planning a stay or activity.

ACCOMMODATIONS

There are all kinds of accommodations in Lake George. As a rule, Lake George is not a discount destination, but most travelers can find a hotel, motel or inn to meet their needs. Following is a sampling of guest room establishments in the area. Some are convenient to the attractions in Lake George Village, while others offer spectacular lake views and private beaches.

ADMIRAL MOTEL

(401 Canada St. ☎ 518.668.2097 🖰 admiralmotel.com) The Admiral Motel is known as a friendly, clean motel located in the center of Lake George Village. The motel is within walking distance to shopping, dining and other Lake George attractions. Regular and deluxe rooms are available. There is a heated swimming pool, and wireless Internet access too. ($/$$)

DEPE DENE RESORT

(3494 Lake Shore Dr. ☎ 518.668.2788 🖱 depedene.com) The Depe Dene Resort is a waterfront resort in Lake George. The resort offers many activities, including waterskiing, fishing, tennis, wave runner rentals, kayaking, canoeing and horseback riding. Accommodations range from motel rooms to lakefront townhomes. ($$)

HERITAGE OF LAKE GEORGE MOTEL

(419 Canada St. ☎ 518.668.3357 🖱 heritageoflakegeorge.com) The Heritage of Lake George Motel has both motel rooms and small cottages. The establishment is family owned and operated and offers clean accommodations in a central Lake George Village location. ($$)

HOLIDAY INN RESORT AT LAKE GEORGE

(2223 Canada St. ☎ 518.668.5781 🖱 lakegeorgeturf.com) The Holiday Inn Resort at Lake George is a clean, well-maintained hotel on Route 9 in Lake George. It is family owned and offers friendly, personalized service and many updates in its 129-room facility. The hotel is known to be accommodating for families with young children, yet offers a large meeting room for weddings, business gatherings and celebrations. There is also a "club room" for smaller get-togethers. The hotel offers heated indoor and outdoor pools, complimentary high-speed Internet, a whirlpool and sauna, on-site fitness center, and a full service restaurant and lounge. ($$/$$$)

LIDO MOTEL

(1 Old Post Rd. ☎ 518.668.5474 🖱 lidomotel.net) The Lido Motel offers clean accommodations and friendly service in the heart of Lake George Village. The motel is convenient to village attractions and many are within walking distance. ($/$$)

MOHICAN RESORT MOTEL

(1545 State Rte 9 ☎ 518.792.0474 📞 mohicanmotel.com) The Mohican Resort Motel is an established motel with a variety of accommodations including family units and townhouses. It is located between Lake George Village, the **Factory Outlets of Lake George** and **The Great Escape** theme park. The motel is family owned and operated. ($/$$)

SIX FLAGS GREAT ESCAPE LODGE AND INDOOR WATER PARK

(89 Six Flags Dr., Queensbury ☎ 518.824.6060 📞 sixflags.com) The Six Flags Great Escape Lodge and Indoor Water Park is the official resort of **The Great Escape.** Conveniently located across from The Great Escape and Splashwater Kingdom theme park, the lodge offers 200 suites and a 38,000-square-foot indoor water park. The lodge is open all year and features Adirondack-style décor. ($$/$$$)

SUN CASTLE RESORT

(3178 Lake Shore Dr. ☎ 518.668.2085 📞 suncastleresort.com) Sun Castle Resort is a waterfront resort offering two bedroom townhouse and villa accommodations. The resort sits on 15 acres and has its own private beach. Private boat docking is available. Weekly and daily rates are available. ($$)

TALL PINES MOTEL

(1747 State Rte 9 ☎ 518.668.5122 📞 tallpinesmotel.com) Tall Pines Motel is a family owned and run motel located between

Lake George Village and The Great Escape theme park. The rooms are clean and the service is friendly. All rooms include a deck, and access to a heated outdoor pool, Jacuzzi, sauna and barbeques. ($$)

THE BOULDERS RESORT
(3036 Lake Shore Dr. ☎ 518.668.5444 ☗ bouldersresort.com)
The Boulders Resort is a pleasant lakefront resort on Lake George offering cottages, townhomes and motel guest rooms. Located less than a mile from Lake George Village, the resort is close to shopping, restaurants and area attractions. Most rooms have a lake view. Amenities include a sandy beach, boat dock, picnic areas, multiple pools, hot tub, game room and playground. Guests also have free access to kayaks, paddleboats, canoes and rowboats. ($$)

THE INN AT ERLOWEST
(3178 Lake Shore Dr. ☎ 518.668.2085 ☗ theinnaterlowest.com)
The Inn at Erlowest is a waterfront estate inn on Lake George that was built in 1898. It shares the property of the **Sun Castle Resort** and offers stunning views of the lake from the large stone "castle." The inn offers 10 guest rooms, an event and meeting facility, and a dining room. ($$$)

THE LODGES AT CRESTHAVEN ✪ Must See!
(3210 Lake Shore Dr. ☎ 518.668.3332 ☗ lakegeorgelodges.com)
The Lodges at Cresthaven offer beautiful Adirondack-style guest accommodations with two bedrooms, two bathrooms, kitchens, washer and dryer, entertainment centers and lakefront views. There is a restaurant and bar on site, and a sandy beach with a swimming area. Other amenities include an indoor-

outdoor pool, fitness room, game room, grocery delivery service, outdoor game courts and fishing. The facility can also host weddings and other events. Nightly and weekly rates are available, although minimum stays are required during peak seasons. ($$)

CAMPING

There are a handful of nice camping facilities near Lake George Village. Campgrounds with tent sites, hookups and cabin facilities are all within an easy drive from the main attractions in town. Facilities fill up quickly during prime time, so visitors should call ahead for reservations.

ADIRONDACK CAMPING VILLAGE
(43 Finkle Rd. ☎ 518.668.5226

📎 adirondackcampingvillage.com) The Adirondack Camping Village is a family-operated camping facility located less than a five-minute drive to Lake George Village and the lake itself. Nestled in the woods, the campground offers tent sites, full hookups, 50-amp cable sites, restrooms, hot showers, laundry facilities, a camp store, dump station, heated pool, game room and nature trails.

From the Northway (I-87), take exit 23. Turn left on Diamond Point Road, and then turn left at the traffic light at the intersection of Route 9 and Diamond Point Road. Continue two miles south on Route 9. The campground is on the left. ($)

HEARTHSTONE POINT CAMPGROUND

(3298 Lake Shore Dr. ☎ 518.668.5193

⬤ dec.ny.gov/outdoor/24470.html) Hearthstone Point
Campground is a New York State campground located on
Lake George. At just two miles from Lake George Village, it is
an accessible and convenient facility. There are 13 campsites,
picnic tables, showers, restrooms and a gazebo.

From the Northway (I-87), take exit 22 to Route 9N. Continue
two miles to the campground (on the right). ($)

LAKE GEORGE BATTLEGROUND CAMPGROUND

(2224 State Rte 9 ☎ 518.668.3348

⬤ dec.ny.gov/outdoor/24453.html) Lake George Battleground
Campground is a New York State campground located just a
quarter of a mile south of Lake George Village. History buffs
may be especially interested in this facility since it is close to
many historical sights. Campers can visit the Lake George
Battleground or take a self-guided interpretive historical path
that provides information at the Battlefield Park.

There are 68 tent and trailer sites, hot showers, flush toilets,
a trailer dump station, a recycle center and mobility-impaired
accessibility.

From the Northway (I-87), take exit 21 to Route 9N. Continue
approximately one mile to the campground on the right. ($)

LAKE GEORGE ESCAPE CAMPING RESORT

(175 East Schroon River Rd. ☎ 518.623.3207

⬤ lakegeorgeescape.com) The Lake George Escape Camping
Resort is located on 175 acres and one mile of waterfront on

the Schroon River, Frog Pond and Moose Pond. They offer 575 RV sites and more than 100 tent sites. Rental units and camping cabins are also available. Pets are welcome with some restrictions. The campground is known for offering many family and outdoor activities, and for having friendly staff. ($$)

LAKE GEORGE ISLAND CAMPING
(Glen Island ☎ 518.644.9696, Long Island ☎ 518.656.9426, Narrow Island ☎ 518.499.1288
📍 dec.ny.gov/outdoor/24474.html) There are three groups of islands on Lake George—Glen, Long and Narrow. The islands are widely scattered on the lake and offer nicely located state-run campsites. All sites are only accessible by boat, and no dogs are allowed. There is a separate headquarters for each island group. Reservations are required. ($)

DINING

There are dozens and dozens of restaurants to choose from in Lake George. Steak and ribs are popular choices in the village, as is fresh seafood. Most restaurants offer casual dining and are family friendly. In general, the restaurants are service oriented and do a good job taking care of their guests. Although some establishments have remained for decades and survive off of repeat customers who return year after year, enough new restaurants spring up from time to time to keep things interesting.

ADIRONDACK PUB & BREWERY
(33 Canada St. ☎ 518.668.0002 📍 adkpub.com) The Adirondack Pub & Brewery is a fun place to have a casual meal and local beer. The atmosphere is upbeat and in the spirit of

the Adirondacks. The establishment is "first and foremost" a brewpub and offers handcrafted ales such as the Bear Naked Ale, Snow Trout Stout, and Hunter Mountain Hefeweizen. The food menu includes traditional pub fare such as burgers, fish and chips, and sandwiches. Kids are welcome and takeout is available. ($/$$)

BARNSIDER SMOKEHOUSE RESTAURANT

(2112 State Rte 9 ☎ 518.668.5268 ● barnsider.com) The Barnsider prides itself in having "Serious Barbeque" and that is what they've been known for since 1991. They offer Memphis-style barbeque as well as steaks, seafood and sandwiches. The ribs are highly acclaimed and "all you can eat" rib night is legendary. ($/$$)

BOATHOUSE RESTAURANT

(3210 Lake Shore Dr. ☎ 518.668.2389) The Boathouse Restaurant offers great lakefront views and a relaxing atmosphere on Lake George. They offer a wide menu with steaks, burgers, seafood and salads. They also have nightly chef's specials. ($$)

CAFFE VERO

(185 Canada St. ☎ 518.668.5800 ● caffeverocoffee.com) Caffe Vero is a pleasant, well-run coffee house in Lake George. They serve a limited breakfast menu with thick bread and fluffy pancakes, and offer service with a smile. The coffee is excellent and reasonably priced. They offer baked goods for eat-in or takeout. ($)

DUFFY'S TAVERN

(20 Amherst St. ☎ 518.668.5323) Duffy's Tavern is open year-round. During the season and for Winter Carnival, they feature lake views and live entertainment. Their menu includes casual items such as burgers, homemade soup, grilled sandwiches and wings. The tavern is located on the corner of Amherst Street and Canada Street. ($)

FARMHOUSE RESTAURANT

(Top of the World Golf Resort, 441 Lockhart Mountain Rd. ☎ 518.668.3000 🌐 topoftheworldgolfresort.com) The Farmhouse Restaurant at the **Top of the World Golf Resort** is located in a renovated 19th century dining room. The menu includes organic seasonal ingredients and the offerings change regularly. They serve lunch and dinner, and have special family-style Harvest Dinners on Thursdays. Reservations are accepted. ($$)

THE INN AT ERLOWEST

(3178 Lake Shore Dr. ☎ 518.668.2085 🌐 theinnaterlowest.com) The Inn at Erlowest offers a charming dining facility on the Lake George waterfront. Their menu includes seafood, steaks and specialty dishes. The food preparation is beautiful, and they offer good wine pairings. The staff is professional, friendly and attentive without being aggressive. A nice place to celebrate a special occasion—and when the weather is nice, it's hard to top a meal on the large lake view patio. ($$/$$$)

LOG JAM RESTAURANT

(Rte 9 and Rte 149 ☎ 518.798.1155 🌐 logjamrestaurant.com) The Log Jam Restaurant is a staple in Lake George. Its roots go back to 1951, and the current chef has been there since 1989. The Log Jam offers casual dining for lunch and dinner in a cozy log cabin. They are known for their prime rib but offer many other items and daily features. Light pub fare is available in the lounge between lunch and dinner. Reservations are accepted. ($/$$)

LONE BULL PANCAKE AND STEAK HOUSE
(3502 Lake Shore Dr. ☎ 518.668.5703) The Lone Bull Pancake and Steak House is a solid bet for a good family breakfast. It offers friendly but no-frills service, good eggs and pancakes, and reasonable prices. ($)

PIZZA JERKS
(59 Iroquois St. ☎ 518.668.4411 ☗ pizzajerks.com) Pizza Jerks is a casual dine-in, carry out and delivery New York–style pizzeria. They offer pizza, calzone, stromboli, garlic knots, salads and desserts. Their menu includes some original pizza combinations such as the "Carcass" meat pizza and the "Tree Hugger" veggie pizza. ($)

PORRECA'S RESTAURANT
(2897 Lake Shore Dr. ☎ 518.668.5259
☗ nordicks.com/restaurant.asp) Porreca's Restaurant is a small Italian restaurant located at the northern end of Lake George Village. They are located in the Nordick's Motel and they serve breakfast and dinner. Their entrees are original and include delicious homemade pasta specials such as ravioli stuffed with unique fillings. The desserts are also worth a try. The restaurant can be a quiet alternative to some of the larger establishments during peak season. ($/$$)

RAIN TREE RESTAURANT

(3259 Lake Shore Dr. ☎ 518.668.3900 🖱 theraintree.com) It's difficult to pass up a meal in the cozy log cabin of the Rain Tree Restaurant. The restaurant has a wide menu of fine dining, casual fare, pub food and desserts. There is a full bar and large stone fireplace in the dining room, or enjoy the terrace for warm weather dining. ($/$$)

SMOKEY JOE'S SALOON & GRILL

(25 Canada St. ☎ 518.668.2660

🖱 smokeyjoessaloonandgrill.com) Smokey Joe's Saloon & Grill offers a rustic atmosphere and stick-to-your-bones food such as award-winning barbeque ribs, brisket, wraps, pulled pork and their own pizzadillas. Try the "deal for two" full rack of ribs for the full Smokey Joe's experience. The staff is friendly and there's a bar, happy hour specials on weeknights, and a children's menu. ($/$$)

ATTRACTIONS

The phrase "there is something for everyone" may be widely overused, but Lake George is a tourist town of contrasts and as such, offers a wide variety of visitor attractions. The sheer beauty of the Adirondacks and Lake George itself is ever-present in and around the village, but there is also a heavy theme park element, and even something for history buffs.

ADIRONDACK EXTREME ADVENTURE COURSE

(35 Westwood Forest Ln., Bolton Landing ☎ 518.494.7200
🖱 adirondackextreme.com) The Adirondack Extreme Adventure Course is a treetop adventure park for adults and kids located

in Bolton Landing (10 minutes north of Lake George). The park offers multiple aerial courses containing zip lines, scrambling walls, bridges, rope swings and hanging nets. ($$)

ADVENTURE FAMILY FUN CENTER

(1079 Lake George Rd., Queensbury ☎ 518.798.7860 ⬤ gocartslakegeorge.com) The Adventure Family Fun Center is located just south of **The Great Escape** and offers a large outdoor go-kart track, indoor go-kart track, bumper cars, paintball, laser tag, arcade games, rock climbing and a bungee-jump trampoline. The facility is open year-round and offers group rates for parties. ($/$$)

FACTORY OUTLETS OF LAKE GEORGE

(1444 State Rte 9 ⬤ factoryoutletsoflakegeorge.com) Within a half-mile area in Lake George, there are four major outlet shopping centers—French Mountain Commons, Adirondack Outlet Mall, Log Jam Outlet Center, and Lake George Plaza. There are more than 70 stores.

FORT WILLIAM HENRY MUSEUM

(50 Canada St. ☎ 518.668.5471 ⬤ fwhmuseum.com) History buffs may enjoy the Fort William Henry Museum, which is open seasonally in Lake George. The fort sits on a small hill and was the command center for the southern end of Lake George for two years during the French and Indian War (aka the Seven Years' War). The museum offers educational programs, a store, special events and ghost tours. ($)

THE GREAT ESCAPE AND SPLASHWATER KINGDOM
(1172 State Rte 9, Queensbury ☎ 518.792.3500

⬤ sixflags.com) The Great Escape and Splashwater Kingdom is a Six Flags theme park that is perhaps the biggest attraction in the Lake George area aside from the lake itself. The park, located at exit 20 on the Northway (Route 87) is really two theme parks in one and offers more than 135 rides. The Great Escape, with everything from thrilling roller coasters to family rides, is a traditional amusement park. The second, Splashwater Kingdom, is a waterpark where guests can wear their bathing suits and spend the day getting wet.

Thrill-seekers won't be disappointed with the rides at The Great Escape. Some of the wildest rides in the country live at the park, including a few record-holders. Ride an 80-year-old wooden roller coaster, The Comet, or drop 192 feet in Sasquatch, the park's terrifying drop tower. Other rides include names such as Steamin' Demon, Alpine Bobsled, and the Boomerang Coast to Coaster.

Splashwater Kingdom is all about getting wet. With a huge wave pool, multiple waterslides and many unique water rides, visitors don't have time to dry off, nor do they want to. Drop through a 100-foot tunnel and take a swirl around a giant bowl before being tossed into the water on Mega Wedgie or dodge water canyons as you ride down the 1,100 foot Captain Hook's Adventure River. The question most visitors ask is not "which one" but "which one first"?

Great Escape and Splashwater Kingdom operate under different hours. Both are seasonal. Splashwater Kingdom is only open from Memorial Day through Labor Day, while

The Great Escape maintains weekend hours in the shoulder seasons. On-site accommodations are available at the Great Escape Lodge and Indoor Waterpark. Daily and seasonal passes area available. ($$)

HOUSE OF FRANKENSTEIN WAX MUSEUM

(213 Canada St. ☎ 518.668.3377

☗ frankensteinwaxmuseum.com) A classic in Lake George since the 1970s, not much has changed at the House of Frankenstein Wax Museum. More than 50 exhibits of horror come to life, as guests interact and react to haunting figures and scenes throughout the museum. The House of Frankenstein Wax Museum is located in the center of Lake George Village on Canada Street. The museum is open seasonally. ($)

LAKE GEORGE DINNER THEATRE

(Holiday Inn Resort Lake George, 2223 Canada St.

☎ 518.668.5762 x411 ☗ lakegeorgedinnertheatre.com) Dinner and a show, the old-fashioned way, is what visitors to the Lake George Dinner Theatre can expect and enjoy. The price of a ticket includes tableside service, a choice of entrees and an evening (or afternoon) of professional live entertainment. Visitors should consult the theatre's website for a current show schedule. The theatre is located in the **Holiday Inn Resort Lake George**. ($$)

LAKE GEORGE STEAMBOAT COMPANY

(57 Beach Rd. ☎ 518.668.5777

☗ lakegeorgesteamboat.com) The Lake George Steamboat Company offers a unique perspective on Lake George from aboard a stern-wheel steamboat. Steamboats have a long history on Lake George and cruises of various lengths are available on a choice of three ships. Complete historic tours are offered as well as scenic hour-long outings. Charters are also available. ($/$$)

NATURAL STONE BRIDGE & CAVE PARK

(535 Stone Bridge Rd., Pottersville ☎ 518.494.2283 📱 stonebridgeandcaves.com) Natural Stone Bridge and Cave Park boasts the largest marble cave entrance in the East. Visitors take a self-guided hike to explore caves, waterfalls and a gorge. The privately run park also features guided adventure tours, Frisbee golf, climbing walls and gemstone mining. There is a large rock shop on site as well. The park is located 23 miles north of Lake George in Pottersville. It is open year-round and offers snowshoeing in winter. ($)

PROSPECT MOUNTAIN

(Intersection of Rte 9 and Rte 9N) Prospect Mountain Veterans Memorial Parkway offers a scenic five-mile drive up Prospect Mountain. There are three overlooks along the way and visitors are rewarded with a wonderful 100-mile view from the top. Sites from the top—where there's a picnic area—include Lake George and the Green Mountains in Vermont. Trolley service to the top is available, as well as a somewhat challenging hiking trail. The view in the fall is no less than spectacular. There is a nominal fee per car. ($)

SADDLE UP STABLES

(Lake Shore Dr. ☎ 518.668.4801 📱 ridingstables.com) Saddle Up Stables is located three miles north of Lake George Village. They offer scenic Western-style trail rides overlooking Lake

George. Guests must be at least six years old and 48 inches tall. The stable is open seasonally. ($$)

TOP OF THE WORLD GOLF COURSE

(441 Lockhart Mountain Rd. ☎ 518.668.3000
⬤ **topoftheworldgolfresort.com)** The Top of the World Golf Course offers a challenging 18-hole course set against the beautiful Adirondack scenery. The course is located on French Mountain. From the top, it's easy to see Lake George and the Vermont mountains. ($$)

BEACHES

There are three main beaches in Lake George: Million Dollar Beach, Shepard's Park Beach and Usher's Park Beach.

MILLION DOLLAR BEACH

The most popular beach in Lake George is Million Dollar Beach. It is located at the bottom of Lake George just past the steamboats. The State of New York runs the beach and it is well maintained and clean. There is no admission fee for the beach but there is a parking fee. There are changing facilities, volleyball courts and lovely sand on the beach. Million Dollar Beach is very crowded in peak season.

SHEPARD'S PARK BEACH

Shepard's Park Beach is located right in the village on Canada Street behind the fountain and stage. The beach is free, and there are restrooms. It is conveniently located close to restaurants and shopping.

USHER'S PARK BEACH

On Route 9L, just past Million Dollar Beach is a quiet, free beach called Usher's Park Beach. Located off the parking lot and down a hill, this beach is nice for families with small children since it is much quieter than the other beaches. There is a lifeguard on duty as well and the water in the swim area is very shallow. Usher's Park Beach also has a playground and picnic area.

FESTIVALS AND EVENTS

There are many annual festivals, carnivals, exhibits and events in Lake George and the surrounding area.

ADIRONDACK BALLOON FESTIVAL

(Floyd Bennett Memorial Airport, Queensbury ☎ 518.792.2600 ☗ lakegeorge.com) The Adirondack Balloon Festival is an annual event dating back more than 35 years. The festival takes place at the end of September and is one of the premier festivals in the Lake George area. Hundreds of hot air balloons participate and most take off from the Floyd Bennett Memorial Airport. The airport is located three miles northeast of the downtown area of Glens Falls, off Quaker Road in the Town of Queensbury. Admission is free for spectators.

AMERICADE MOTORCYCLE RALLY

(☗ lakegeorge.com/americade/info.cfm) Each June, Lake George plays host to the world's biggest multibrand motorcycle touring rally. The Americade brings more than 50,000 attendees and vendors to Lake George for six days of events and exhibits.

ANNUAL ANTIQUE TRUCK SHOW

(Saratoga County Fairgrounds, Ballston Spa ☎ 518.893.7804)
The Mohawk chapter of the American Truck Historical Society Truck Show holds the Annual Antique Truck Show at the end of September at the Saratoga County Fairgrounds. More than 300 trucks participate each year. The show features trucks of all sizes, tractors and engines. There is a nominal fee for admission. The show is held rain or shine.

ELVIS FEST

(☎ 518.681.7452 🖱 lakegeorgeelvisfest.com) The LakeGeorge.com Elvis Festival is held each June in Lake George. Since its inception in 2004, the festival has become the second-largest Elvis Tribute Artist Competition in the world. Competitors and spectators from around the country and the world participate in the three-day competition. More than 100 volunteers assist in the production of the festival each year.

FRIGHT FEST

(The Great Escape, 1172 State Rte 9, Queensbury ☎ 518.792.3500) Throughout the month of October on the weekends, **The Great Escape** holds Fright Fest. Ghoulish shows, children's events, haunted houses and street decorations throughout the park are geared toward putting visitors in a Halloween mood. There is even trick or treating. ($$)

LAKE GEORGE OKTOBERFEST

(Adirondack Pub & Brewery, 33 Canada St. ☎ 518.668.0002)
In mid-October, the Lake George Oktoberfest is held at the **Adirondack Pub & Brewery**. Attendees are encouraged to wear Oktoberfest costumes. Special events include micro-brew

tasting and live German music. Authentic German food is served. Tickets may be purchased ahead of time or at the door.

WINTER CARNIVAL

Winter Carnival is a 50-plus-year tradition in Lake George. It is held each weekend in February and kicks off with opening ceremonies at the park beach. The carnival includes activities throughout the village such as parades, sports competitions, cook-offs, bonfires, dog sled rides and fireworks. Many local businesses participate in the carnival and offer special meals and/or services in celebration of the event. A schedule of events is distributed each year throughout town.

Old Forge

Old Forge is a popular Adirondack destination for people living in western New York. A thriving tourist town in its own right, Old Forge offers many summer and winter activities. Located 98 miles southwest of Lake Placid, Old Forge is only an hour's drive from Utica, two hours from Syracuse, and four hours from Buffalo.

Old Forge has a friendly, comfortable vibe. It is distinctly Adirondack, with many rustic buildings in town. Most activities in the area are centered on the outdoors, but it also has desirable amenities for visitors at reasonable prices. Many vacationers in Old Forge return year after year. Families grow up visiting the town and, generation after generation, return each year to their home away from home.

SUMMER ACTIVITIES

Old Forge bustles in the summer. Vacationers come for the beautiful lakes, mountains, golf courses, hiking trails, mountain biking, boating and canoeing. Old Forge is a traditional Adirondack town, and visitors seeking outdoor adventure in a rustic mountain setting will enjoy the town and its long history.

WINTER IN OLD FORGE

Old Forge is a four-season destination. Although the peak time for tourists is in the summer, winter also draws visitors looking for outdoor fun. Five-hundred miles of groomed snowmobile trails and lots of cross-country ski trails bring people outside and into the woods all winter. A small downhill ski area, McCauley Mountain, is also located just outside of town.

ACCOMMODATIONS

Accommodations to suit most tastes are available in and around Old Forge. Many establishments were constructed decades ago, but their warmth, charm and desirable locations are still fresh today.

19TH GREEN MOTEL

(2761 State Rte 28 ☎ 315.369.3575 🛈 19thgreenmotel.com)
The 19th Green Motel is located less than half a mile south of Old Forge on Route 28. They offer clean, comfortable motel rooms with one or two queen beds. The motel, family owned and run, has been operating for more than 20 years. The 19th Green is close to shopping and restaurants, and the owners are friendly and accommodating. ($/$$)

CHRISTY'S MOTEL

(2902 State Rte 28 ☎ 315.369.6138 🛈 christysmotel.com)
Christy's is a clean, family-oriented motel that is centrally located on Main Street in Old Forge. The rooms are spacious, the staff is friendly and the rates are reasonable. Christy's is open all year and caters to snowmobilers in winter. It is within walking distance of many shops and restaurants. ($/$$)

COUNTRY CLUB MOTEL

(Rte 28 ☎ 315.369.6340 🛈 ccmoldforge.com) The Country Club Motel offers well-maintained facilities close to some of Old Forge's primary attractions such as the **Enchanted Forest/Water Safari** park. The staff is friendly, and the rooms are clean and comfortable. Room prices are very reasonable. ($/$$)

FORGE MOTEL

(104 Lamberton St. ☎ 315.369.3313 🖱 forgemotel.net) The Forge Motel overlooks Old Forge Lake, and is within easy walking distance to many shops, restaurants and attractions in the town. Open year-round, the motel offers simple but comfortable rooms with lake views. Amenities include private patios, lake and mountain views and an indoor heated pool. The service at the motel is friendly, and the rates are reasonable. ($/$$)

NORTH WOODS INN

(4920 State Rte 28 Fourth Lake ☎ 315.369.6777 🖱 northwoodsinnresort.com) The North Woods Inn is a four-season waterfront resort located on Fourth Lake in Old Forge. They offer lodging in rooms or cabins and have two dining facilities on site. They can also host weddings and other events. ($$)

PINE KNOLL LODGE AND CABINS

(123 S. Shore Rd. ☎ 315.369.6740 🖱 pineknolllodge.net) Pine Knoll Lodge and Cabins overlooks Old Forge Lake, and offers guests pleasant and scenic accommodations. The facility is located a short distance off the main tourist area of Old Forge but within walking distance of stores and restaurants. They have a private beach, and accommodations include standard rooms, rooms with kitchenettes and cabins. The owners are friendly and gracious hosts, and the rooms are well maintained and clean. ($$)

VILLAGE COTTAGES

(156 Garmon Ave. ☎ 315.369.3432 ▯ villagecottages.com) The Village Cottages offer eight all-season cottages that can house between two and ten people. The cottages rent by the weekend, week or entire season. The Village Cottages are located a short walk from Main Street in a quiet neighborhood. The owners are friendly and attentive to the property and continually make upgrades and improvements to the property. ($$)

WATER'S EDGE INN & CONFERENCE CENTER

(3188 State Rte 28 ☎ 315.369.2484 ▯ watersedgeinn.com) The Water's Edge Inn & Conference Center is located on the waterfront in Old Forge. It is one of the largest and most easily recognizable hotels in Old Forge. The facility offers nice views, a conference center and a private dock for guest use. The hotel is open all year and offers a variety of accommodations. ($$)

CAMPING

Camping is a big activity in the Old Forge area. There are several campgrounds just outside of town to accommodate most camping needs. Campgrounds fill up quickly in the summer months, so visitors should plan ahead and make reservations.

OLD FORGE CAMPING RESORT

(3347 State Rte 28 ☎ 315.369.6011 ▯ oldforgecamping.com) The Old Forge Camping Resort is a four-season campground offering tent sites, RV camping, cottage rentals and log cabin rentals. Amenities include seven heated restroom and shower facilities, a main lodge, convenience store, laundry facilities, arcade and family lounge. Electric sites, cabins and cottages are available to rent at reasonable rates for the entire winter season. ($)

NICK'S LAKE CAMPGROUND

(278 Bisby Rd. ☎ 315.369.3314

☻ dec.ny.gov/outdoor/24485.html) Nick's Lake Campground is a very nice New York State–run facility located in the Black River Wild Forest. It has 112 campsites, a picnic area, a large beach on the lake with lifeguards, and five miles of hiking trails. There are clean, modern bathrooms in multiple locations around the campground with hot showers. The 205-acre lake is open to nonmotorized vehicles only. ($)

SINGING WATERS CAMPGROUND

(☎ 315.369.6618 ☻ singingwaterscamp.com) Singing Waters Campground has 150 camping sites (75 with full hookups, 57 with electric and water, and 18 tent sites). They are open year-round and offer heated, winterized, rustic six-person cabins with two rooms, a loft and a small kitchen. Winter rentals are available. ($)

DINING

Most dining options in Old Forge are casual in nature and privately owned. Patrons don't normally need to worry about showing up to eat in outdoor clothes after a long day in the wilderness. Most establishments are friendly, and restaurant owners generally go out of their way to make guests feel welcome.

ADIRONDACK PIZZERIA

(Main St. ☎ 315.369.6028) The Adirondack Pizzeria serves dine-in and take-out pizza, wings and subs. They also have an arcade on site. ($)

BILLY'S

(Main St., in the Fern's complex ☎ 315.369.2001) Billy's is an Italian American restaurant located on Main Street in Old Forge. Visitors enjoy a comfortable, relaxed atmosphere and service with a smile. The food is dependable and the portions substantial. Warm crusty bread, fresh homemade pasta and good house specialties are just some of the reasons visitors return. ($/$$)

DAIKER'S INN

(157 Daikers Circle ☎ 315.369.6954) Daiker's Inn offers a pleasant dining atmosphere on Fourth Lake. There's a nice deck with a view and courteous staff. The food is casual but good. Daiker's Inn is a fine choice for a place to kick back after a long day outdoors. ($/$$)

FRANKIE'S TASTE OF ITALY

(2824 State Rte 28 ☎ 315.369.2400 🖰 frankiesitalianfood.com) Frankie's is Old Forge's original Italian restaurant. They are known for their delicious bread and traditional Italian dishes. The menu is large, the portions are generous and the food is satisfying. The bread pudding is a local favorite. ($/$$)

MAIN STREET STATION

(2963 Rte 28 ☎ 315.369.1100) Main Street Station is a casual pizza and sandwich shop located on Route 28 (near the edge of town). The interior is very modest, but the subs are made fresh right in front of you on thick homemade bread, and the staff is normally chatty and warm. They serve pizza, hoagies, subs, wraps, Stromboli and salads.

RANDY'S RESTAURANT

(2918 State Rte 28 ☎ 315.369.2888 📍 randys-restaurant.com)
Visitors looking for comfort food can find a variety of core-warming, home-style entrees at Randy's. Chili, meat loaf and mashed potatoes can take the chill out of a long day in the snow. Randy's is small, reasonably priced and a favorite of many local residents. They offer a popular fish fry every Friday night. Takeout is available. ($/$$)

SISTERS BISTRO ✪ Must See!

(3046 Main St. ☎ 315.369.1053 📍 sistersbistro.com) Healthy food, beautiful presentation and seasonal menu items make Sisters Bistro a popular choice for "small plates" dining in Old Forge. Located in an attractively restored Victorian home, they use fresh, mostly local ingredients and have many vegetarian options. Prices aren't cheap but the food is prepared well. Seating is available in the dining room, at the antique bar, on the front porch and on the rear deck. Sisters Bistro is a nice change of pace for dining in the Adirondacks. They also have an extensive wine list. ($$)

SLICKERS

(3132 Main St. ☎ 315.369.3002) Slickers is a lively, casual restaurant serving lunch and dinner near the lakefront on Main Street. It offers a fun pub atmosphere and a good variety of menu items such as burgers, pasta, sandwiches and salads.

There are a couple of video games and a pool table, and the wait staff and bartenders are usually outgoing. Slickers is a good place to grab a beer and socialize, and a fun place to bring the family as well. ($/$$)

ATTRACTIONS AND ACTIVITIES

Old Forge is full of attractions and activities for the entire family. Aside from the obvious outdoor pursuits that many visitors come for, Old Forge offers arts and entertainment for people of all ages.

ARTS CENTER/OLD FORGE
(3260 State Rte 28 ☎ 315.369.6411 ♦ artscenteroldforge.org)
The Arts Center/Old Forge offers regional and national exhibitions, performances, lectures and workshops. They also organize fitness and cooking classes, and sponsor many festivals in Old Forge. Visitors can review a schedule of upcoming events on the center's website.

CALYPSO'S COVE FAMILY ENTERTAINMENT CENTER
(3183 State Rte 28 ☎ 315.369.6145 ♦ calypsoscove.com)
Calypso's Cove Family Entertainment Center offers go-karts, bumper boats, a rock climbing wall, miniature golf, batting cages and an arcade. It is located next to the **Enchanted Forest/Water Safari** on Route 28. ($/$$)

ENCHANTED FOREST/WATER SAFARI
(3188 State Rte 28 ☎ 315.369.6145 ♦ watersafari.com) The Enchanted Forest/Water Safari is one of New York's largest water theme parks. Open mid-June through early September,

the park has been in operation for more than 50 years, and boasts more than 50 rides and attractions (32 are water rides). The Enchanted Forest/Water Safari offers water slides, splash rides, traditional amusement park rides, food, games and theme characters. ($/$$)

KAYAK AND CANOE RENTALS

(Mountainman Outdoor Supply Company, Rte 28 ☎ 315.369.6672 ▮ mountainmanoutdoors.com) Mountainman Outdoor Supply Company says they are New York's largest canoe and kayak dealer. This is easy to believe when visitors see firsthand the huge selection of boats offered for sale and rent in their store. As a "complete Adirondack Wilderness Outfitter," the company carries over 1,000 flat and whitewater boats and paddling accessories. Mountainman also sells camping, hiking, biking and winter sporting gear, along with outdoor clothing. Mountainman Outdoor Supply Company also sponsors Paddlefest, America's largest on-water boat sale held each May. ($/$$)

MCCAULEY MOUNTAIN SKI AREA

(Rte 28 ☎ 315.369.3225 ▮ mccauleyny.com) McCauley Mountain Ski Area provides skiers with 21 ski trails and 633 feet of vertical drop on McCauley Mountain. The ski area is located just outside Old Forge off Route 28. The average snow base is more than 120 inches, and they have snow making capabilities for 65% of the trails. Chairlift rides are available in the summer months. ($$)

OLD FORGE LAKE CRUISES

(State Rte 28 and Lakeview Ave. ☎ 315.369.6473) Old Forge Lake Cruises offers narrated sightseeing boat rides through the Fulton Chain of Lakes. Their boats are equipped with snack bars, restrooms and heated lower cabins. Cruises are offered Memorial Day through Columbus Day. ($/$$)

OLD FORGE BEACH AND TENNIS COURTS

(Lake View Ave.) The Old Forge Beach and Tennis Courts are located on the waterfront in Old Forge off Lake View Avenue. There are two tennis courts and a swimming beach with lifeguards. Admission is free and there is parking nearby. The beach is open seven days a week in the summer and can be quite crowded during peak season.

STRAND THEATRE OF OLD FORGE

(Rte 28 ☎ 315.369.2792 🌐 strandoldforge.com) The Strand Theatre originally opened in 1923 as the Thomson Theatre. Today, the Strand Theatre is privately owned and operated and has been beautifully restored. The attention to detail by the current owners, and their love for the building and its history is evident throughout the building. Movie and concession prices are reasonable and the atmosphere is lively and inviting. The theatre is also available for parties and events. ($)

THENDARA GOLF CLUB

(Thendara ☎ 315.369.3136 🌐 thendaragolfclub.com) The Thendara Golf Club near Old Forge offers an 18-hole, par 72, championship golf course designed by Donald Ross. The course was once played by famous golfers such as Jack

Nicklaus and Arnold Palmer. The course was established in 1921 and is open to the public. ($$)

TICKNER'S MOOSE RIVER CANOE TRIPS

(Riverside Ln. ☎ 315.369.6286 ◉ ticknerscanoes.com) Tickner's Moose River Canoe Trips offers half- and full-day float trips on the Moose River. Trips include canoes, life vests, paddles and shuttle service. ($/$$)

FESTIVALS AND EVENTS

Festivals and events take place year-round in Old Forge. No matter what the temperature is outside, people are out and about, and enjoying many community planned events.

ADIRONDACK ICE BOWL

(Pond Hockey Tournament, North Woods Inn Resort, Fourth Lake ◉ adirondackicebowl.com) The Adirondack Ice Bowl is an annual pond hockey tournament that takes place in late January on Fourth Lake in the Fulton Chain of Lakes. The three-day outdoor tournament features more than 50 teams. Lodging is available at tournament rates at the North Woods Inn in Old Forge.

ADIRONDACK NATIONAL EXHIBITION OF AMERICAN WATERCOLORS

(Arts Center/Old Forge, 3260 State Rte 28 ☎ 315.369.6411 ◉ artscenteroldforge.org) The Adirondacks National Exhibition of American Watercolors is an annual event that has been held for more than 30 years. It features works from many of the top living painters in North America. Noted as a highly competitive watercolor exhibition, the event has received many accolades in the art community.

ADIRONDACK POLKA FESTIVAL

(North Street Pavilion, 225 North St. 🖱 **oldforgeny.com)** Each May, Old Forge hosts the Adirondack Polka Festival. Top polka bands from across the country provide entertainment, and Polish and American food is served. The festival is held at the Hiltebrant Recreation Center Pavilion (near the **Enchanted Forest/Water Safari**).

ADIRONDACK STORYTELLING FESTIVAL

(McCauley Mountain Ski Area, 100 McCauley Mountain Rd. ☎ **315.369.6008** 🖱 **oldforgeny.com)** The Adirondack Storytelling Festival is held annually in July. Traditional music, folklore and crafts are demonstrated for children of all ages. Nature walks are also available. The event is hosted by the Old Forge Library. There is a nominal admission fee.

ANNUAL ANTIQUES SHOW & SALE

(225 North St. ☎ **315.369.6411** 🖱 **artscenteroldforge.org)** The Annual Antiques Show & Sale is held at the end of July at the Hiltebrant Recreation Center on North Street. It is sponsored by the **Arts Center/Old Forge** and has a history dating back more than 35 years. A large variety of vendors sell antiques such as rustic furniture, glassware, rugs, silver and collectibles. A nominal entrance fee is charged.

ANTIQUE BOAT SHOW

(Old Forge Lakefront ☎ **315.369.6983** 🖱 **oldforgeny.com)** For more than 20 years, the annual Antique Boat Show has been held on the Old Forge Lakefront in mid-July. More than 50 antique boats are on display during the show and then make their way to First Lake for the traditional boat parade.

CENTRAL ADIRONDACK ART SHOW

(Arts Center/Old Forge, 3260 State Rte 28 ☎ 315.369.6411 🖱 artscenteroldforge.org) The Central Adirondack Art Show is a large regional event with a 60-plus-year history. The exhibit features work from more than 200 artists including paintings, carvings and sculptures. The event runs for one month in the summertime.

FIRST FRIDAY ART WALKS

(Arts Center/Old Forge, 3260 State Rte 28 ☎ 315.369.6411 🖱 artscenteroldforge.org) On the first Friday of every month from June through October, the **Arts Center/Old Forge** sponsors art walks in town. The walks are organized to gain awareness of local arts in the community. Many businesses stay open late to accommodate art lovers and display local work. Maps of participating businesses are available at local merchants involved in the walk.

OLD FORGE FARMERS MARKET

(Park Ave. ☎ 315.369.2313) The Old Forge Farmers Market is open on Friday afternoons from late June through early October. It is held on Park Avenue between Crosby Boulevard and Lamberton Street.

SNODEO

(Old Forge Visitor Information Center ☎ 315.369.6983 🖱 snodeo.com) The Snodeo is a permanent annual snowmobiling event held in Old Forge to kick off the snowmobiling season. It has more than a 30-year history and is sponsored by the Central Adirondack Association. The Snodeo draws local and visiting snowmobilers for a weekend full of activities including a vintage snowmobile show, raffle, Kitt-Cat/120cc races and fireworks. The event is family oriented and includes children's activities.

THUNDER IN OLD FORGE

(North Street Pavilion, 225 North St. ♾ thunderinoldforge.com)
Each June a Central Adirondack Bike Festival, Thunder in Old Forge, is held at the Hiltebrant Recreation Center Pavilion on North Street. Vendors and exhibitors come from near and far to participate in guided rides, parades, custom bike shows, best bike contest and the Blessing of the Bikes. The event is sponsored by the Central Adirondack Association.

WINTER CARNIVAL

(McCauley Mountain Ski Center ♾ oldforgeny.com) The Winter Carnival in the Central Adirondacks is held for one weekend in February at the **McCauley Mountain Ski Center**. Ski races, other competitions, and fireworks are just some of the activities held during the carnival.

Index

5K Downhill Mountain Bike
    Race   150
19th Green Motel   174
511 Gallery   101
Adirondack 540 Bike Race   150
Adirondack Artists Guild   44
Adirondack Balloon Festival   170
Adirondack Camping Village   158
Adirondack Canoe Classic   150
Adirondack Craft Center   44
Adirondack Decorative Arts &
    Crafts   103
Adirondack Equine Center   43, 129
Adirondack Extreme Adventure
    Course   164
Adirondack Fishing Inc.   117
Adirondack Flying Service   27, 42
Adirondack High Peaks Wilderness
    Area   113
Adirondack Ice Bowl   183
Adirondack International
    Mountainfest   52
Adirondack Lakes & Trails   127
Adirondack Museum   37
Adirondack Museum on Main Store
    and Gallery   100
Adirondack National Exhibition of
    American Watercolors   183
Adirondack Popcorn Co.   99
Adirondack Pizzeria   178
Adirondack Polka Festival   184
Adirondack Pub & Brewery   160
Adirondack Rafting Company   127
Adirondack Regional Airport   27
Adirondack Rock and River Guide
    Service, Inc.   114
Adirondack Scenic Railroad   130
Adirondack Scenic Railroad Rail &
    Canoe   130
Adirondack Store   103
Adirondack Storytelling Festival   184
Adirondack Trailways   25
Adirondack Yarns   91
Adirondak Loj   66
Admiral Motel   154
Adventure Family Fun Center   165
Albany International Airport   26
Alpine Adventures, Inc.   115
Americade Motorcycle Rally   170
Ampersand Mountain   123
Amtrak   27
Annual Antiques Show & Sale   184
Annual Antique Truck Show   171
Antique Boat Show   184
Art Devlin's Olympic Motor Inn   56

Artisans - Lake Placid Lodge   80
Arts Center/Old Forge   180
ArtWalk in Saranac Lake   50
Ashley's Café   75
Ausable Inn Diner   87
Ausable River Two-Fly
    Challenge   144
Avalanche Adventures   47
Bag Time / Lake Placid Clock &
    Watch Co.   92
Balanced Bodywork & Massage of
    Lake Placid   107
Banff Mountain Film Festival   53
Barnsider Smokehouse
    Restaurant   161
Bazzi's Pizzeria   76
Bear Cub Adventure Tours   110
Beglin's Lake Placid Jewelry &
    Gifts   92
Best Western Adirondack Inn   57
Billy's   178
Bloomingdale Bog   114, 126
Bluseed Studios   45
Boathouse Restaurant   161
Bobsledding   140
Body & Sole   92
Bookstore Plus   96
Boulders Resort   157
Bowlwinkles   47
Brown Dog Café & Wine Bar   76
Brush On In   102
Buck Pond   70
Burlington International Airport   26
Caffé Rustica   80
Caffe Vero   161
Calypso's Cove Family Entertainment
    Center   180
Canadian Hockey Enterprises
    Tournaments   33
CAN/AM Hockey Tournaments   33
CAN/AM Rugby Tournament   148
Candy Man   97
Captain Marney's Boat Rentals   112
Caribbean Cowboy   81
Casa del Sol   87
Cascade Lakes Boat Launch   111
Cascade Mountain   122
Cascades Cross-Country Ski
    Center   133
Central Adirondack Art Show   185
Chair 6   81
Christy's Motel   174
Cinderella's   92
Cloudsplitter Mountain Guides
    LLC   115

Index

Cobble Mountain Lodge 60
Coff E Bean Internet Cafe 76
Colby Classic Ice Fishing Derby 144
Cottage at Mirror Lake Inn 85
Country Club Motel 174
Courtyard by Marriott 61
Craig Wood Golf Course 120
Crispin Hair Design & Spa 107
Critters 100
Cross Country Biathlon Center 131, 140
Crowne Plaza 57
Cunningham's Ski Barn 136
Daiker's Inn 178
Dancing Bears 76
Darrah Cooper Jewelers 93
Depe Dene Resort 155
Downhill Grill 82
Duffy's Tavern 162
Eastern Mountain Sports (EMS) 109
Eat 'n Meet Grill and Larder 88
Elvis Fest 171
Emerald Springs Ranch 130
Empire State Winter Games 152
Enchanted Forest/Water Safari 180
Factory Outlets of Lake George 165
Fallen Arch 96
Fanfare of Lake Placid, LLC 100
Farmhouse Restaurant 162
Farmhouse Snowmobiling 139
Festival of Food and Wine 49
Festival of the Colors 51
First Friday Art Walks 185
First Night - Saranac Lake 52
Fish Creek Pond State Campground 70
Flaming Leaves Festival 52
Fly Fish the Adirondacks Guide Service 117
Forge Motel 175
Fortunes of Time 100
Fort William Henry Museum 165
Fowler's Crossing 125
Frankie's Taste of Italy 178
Freaky Friday - Ice Show 32
Fright Fest 171
Generations Restaurant 77
Geology 15
George Jaques Rustic Furniture 104
Glassblowing Shop 96
Golden Arrow Dogsleds 135
Golden Arrow Lakeside Resort 58
Gondola Rides 141
Goose Watch Winery Tasting Room 98
Gore Mountain 136
Grace Camp and Camp Peggy O'Brien 67

Great Adirondack Steak & Seafood Company 77
Great Range Dining 88
Green Goddess Natural Foods 98
Ground Force 1 Limousine & Transportation 30
Guy Brewster Hughes Art Gallery 102
Hearthstone Point Campground 159
Heritage of Lake George Motel 155
High Peaks Cyclery 116
High Peaks Gift Shop 101
High Peaks Guide Service 118
High Peaks Mountain Guides 110
High Peaks Resort 59
Historic Walking Tours 43
Hockey Plus Lake Placid 138
Hohmeyer's Lake Clear Lodge 89
Holiday Inn 155
House of Frankenstein Wax Museum 167
Hungry Trout Fly Shop 118
Hunting, Adirondack Foothills Guide Service 132
I Love BBQ Festival 50
Ice Dance Championships 33
ice skating 138
Imagination Station 93
Inn at Erlowest 157, 162
Int'l Canoe & Kayak Regatta 148
Ironman USA 147
Jackrabbit Trail 134
Jake Placid Doghouse 93
Jay Craft Center 45
John Brown's Farm 38
Johns Brook Lodge 67
Jones Outfitters, LTD. 109
July 4th Parade & Celebration 50
Just Bead It 93
Kayak and Canoe Rentals 181
Keene Farmers Market 106
Lake Colby Boat Launch 112
Lake Flower Boat Launch 112
Lake George Battleground Campground 159
Lake George Dinner Theatre 167
Lake George Escape Camping Resort 159
Lake George Island Camping 160
Lake George Oktoberfest 171
Lake George Steamboat Company 167
Lake Placid Antique Center 94
Lake Placid Boat Launch 112
Lake Placid Boat Tours 42
Lake Placid Center for the Arts 45
Lake Placid Christmas Company 94
Lake Placid Club 18

Lake Placid Club Boat House   86
Lake Placid Club Golf House   83
Lake Placid Club Mountain
    Course   119
Lake Placid Club Resort, Executive
    Course   120
Lake Placid Farmers Market   106
Lake Placid Figure Skating
    Championships   33
Lake Placid Film Forum   49
Lake Placid Horse Show   146
Lake Placid Institute   46
Lake Placid Links Course   119
Lake Placid Lodge   61
Lake Placid Loppet   152
Lake Placid Market   96
Lake Placid Municipal Airport   27
Lake Placid/North Elba Museum   39
Lake Placid Pub & Brewery   83
Lake Placid Sinfonietta   46
Lake Placid Skate Shop   138
Lake Placid Snowmobiling, Inc.   139
Lake Placid Speedy Spa   108
Lake Placid Summer Figure Skating
    Championships   146
Lake Placid Summit Hotel Resort &
    Suites   61
Lake Placid Toboggan Chute   142
Lake Placid Today   21
Lake Placid XPRSS   29
Lido Motel   155
Lisa G's   84
Little Italy   89
Little Whiteface Mountain   128
Lodges at Cresthaven   157
Log Cabin Antiques   94
Log Jam Restaurant   162
Lone Bull Pancake and Steak
    House   163
Long Lake Long Boat Regatta   151
Mac's Canoe Livery   127
Main Street Station   178
Maple Leaf Inn   62
Marathon & Half Marathon   146
Martina's European Skin Care   108
Maui North   136
McCauley Mountain Ski Area   181
Meadowbrook   71
Middle Earth Expeditions   127
Million Dollar Beach   169
Mirror Lake Beach   47
Mirror Lake Boat Launch   112
Mirror Lake Boat Rentals   113
Mirror Lake Inn   63, 108
Mohican Resort Motel   156
Montréal–Pierre Elliott Trudeau
    International Airport   26
Moody Tree Farm   104

Moon Tree Designs   102
Mountain Valley Shuttle   29
Mountain View Inn   59
Mountaineer   115
Mount Baker   123
Mr. Mike's   78
Mt. Jo Hike   121
Mt. Pisgah Ski Center   136
Mt. Van Hoevenberg   122
Natural Stone Bridge & Cave
    Park   168
Newman's News   94
New Year's Masters Ski Jump
    Competition   151
Nick's Lake Campground   177
Nicola's Restaurant Complex   78
Nonna Fina   90
Noon Mark Diner   90
North Pole   48
North Pole Campground and Inn   71
North Woods Inn   60, 175
NYSEF Open Golf
    Tournament   144
Oktoberfest   51
Old Forge Beach and Tennis
    Courts   182
Old Forge Camping Resort   176
Old Forge Farmers Market   185
Old Forge Lake Cruises   182
Olympic Car Show & Parade   51
Olympic Era   19
Olympic Regional Development
    Authority Store   95
Olympic Sports Complex   35, 124,
    134
Paradox Lodge Restaurant & Inn   63
Parking   28
Pat Stratton Memorial Bicycle
    Ride   149
Paul Smith's College   40
Paul Smith's Farmers Market   106
Pine Knoll Lodge and Cabins   175
Pine Pond   125
Pines Inn   65
Pirate's Cove Adventure Golf   48
Pizza Jerks   163
Placid Bay Inn   64
Placid Bay Ventures Outdoor Guide
    Service   118
Placid Life, A   92
Placid Planet Bicycles   116
Point, The   68
Point of View Gallery, A   101
Porreca's Restaurant   163
Prospect Mountain   168
Rain Tree Restaurant   164
Randy's Restaurant   179
Ray Brook Frog   105

Index

Index

Restored Storage Chests   104
Rice Furniture   105
River Rock Salon Inc.   108
Robert Louis Stevenson Cottage and
    Museum   41
Rollins Pond   72
Round the Mountain Canoe and
    Kayak Races   144
Ruthie's Run   95
Saddle Up Stables   168
Saranac Inn Golf Course   120
Saranac Laboratory Museum   41
Saranac Lake Islands   74
Saranac Lake Farmers Market   107
Saranac Sourdough   84
Saturday Night Ice Shows   32
Sheffield Speed Skating Oval   36
Shepard's Park Beach   169
Simply Gourmet/Big Mountain Deli
    & Crêperie   79
Singing Waters Campground   177
Sisters Bistro   179
Six Flags Great Escape Lodge and
    Indoor Water Park   156, 166
Skeleton   141
Slickers   179
Smokey Joe's Saloon & Grill   164
Snodeo   185
Snowshoeing   142
Snow Tours, Inc.   139
Soaring Saturdays   35
Songs at Mirror Lake Music Series   46
Soulshine Bagels   79
South Meadow Farm Lodge   68
South Meadows Farm Maple
    Sugarworks   98
Sparkle Village Arts and Crafts
    Show   53
Stagecoach Inn   62
Strand Theatre of Old Forge   182
St. Regis Canoe Outfitters   128
Sugar Shack Dessert Co.   99
Summer Antiques   95
Summer Ice Skating   132
Summit Lacrosse Tournament   149
Sun Castle Resort   156
Sundowner Series   148
Swedish Hill Winery Tasting
    Room   99
Swiss Acres Inn   64
Tail of the Pup   85
Tall Pines Motel   156
taxi services   30
Temptations from Lake Placid
    Gourmet   99
Thendara Golf Club   182

Thunder in Old Forge   186
Thunder Mountain Dog Sled
    Tours   135
Tibet Asian Himalayan Gifts &
    Handicrafts   97
Tickner's Moose River Canoe
    Trips   183
Titus Mountain   137
Top of the World Golf Course   169
Transformation to a Retreat
    Destination   17
Tupper Lake 9-Miler   146
Twigs Rustic Gallery   105
Two Harts   101
Usher's Park Beach   170
U.S. Olympic Spirit Store   95
U.S. Olympic Training Center   39
V Gallery   102
Veranda   86
Veterans Memorial Hwy   129
View Restaurant   86
Village Comforts   97
Village Cottages   176
Visitor Information Center   23
Water's Edge Inn   176
Wet 'n Wild Wednesdays   34
When to Visit   23
Where'd you get that Hat?   97
Whiteface Club and Resort Golf
    Course   121
Whiteface Lodge   65
Whiteface Mountain   36
Whiteface Mountain Hill Climb Bike
    Race   149
Whiteface Mountain KOA
    Campground   72
Whiteface Mountain Ski Center   124
Whiteface Mountain Uphill Bike
    Race   145
Whiteface Mountain Uphill Foot
    Race   145
Whiteface Ski Resort   137
Wild Center   41
Wilderness Campground at Heart
    Lake   73
Wiley's Flies   118
Wilmington Cross-Country
    Trails   125, 134
Wilmington Notch   73, 113
Winter Carnival   172, 186
Winter Carnival - Saranac Lake   53
Winter in Lake George   154
Winter in Old Forge   173
Winter Olympic Museum   40
XTERRA Lake Placid   148

Other Tourist Town Guides Titles

NAME	ISBN	PRICE
Astoria	978-1-935455-08-0	$14.95
Biloxi	978-1-935455-09-7	$14.95
Black Hills	978-1-935455-10-3	$14.95
Branson	978-1-935455-11-0	$14.95
Deadwood	978-1-935455-22-6	$13.95
Door County	978-1-935455-12-7	$14.95
Fredericksburg	978-1-935455-13-4	$14.95
Key West	978-1-935455-14-1	$14.95
Lake Placid	978-1-935455-15-8	$14.95
Mackinac	978-1-935455-16-5	$14.95
Madison County	978-1-935455-17-2	$13.95
Mystic	978-1-935455-18-9	$14.95
Salem	978-1-935455-19-6	$14.95
Sleepy Hollow	978-1-935455-20-2	$13.95
Solvang	978-1-935455-21-9	$13.95

ORDER FORM

Telephone: With your credit card handy,
call toll-free 800.592.1566

Fax: Send this form toll-free to 866.794.5507

E-mail: Send the information on this form
to orders@channellake.com

Postal mail: Send this form with payment to Channel Lake, Inc.
P.O. Box 1771, New York, NY, 10156

Your Information: ( ) Do not add me to your mailing list

Name: _____

Address: _____

City: _____ State: _____ Zip: _____

Telephone: _____

E-mail: _____

Book Title(s) / ISBN(s) / Quantity / Price
(see www.touristtown.com for this information)

_____

_____

_____

Total payment*: $_____

Payment Information: (Circle One)   Visa / Mastercard

Number: _____ Exp: _____

Or, make check payable to: **Channel Lake, Inc.**

* Add the lesser of $6.50 USD or 18% of the total purchase price for shipping. International orders call or e-mail first! New York orders add 8% sales tax.